Passport to Leadership

(10 Defining Traits and the Leaders Who Lived Them)

by

Bishop Ronnie Hepperly

With

Dr. J. Tod Zeiger

ISBN: 978-1-64288-098-4

Printed in the U.S.A.

ENDORSEMENTS

Ronnie Hepperly is truly a God-called missionary to the nations of the earth. The hurting and helpless are his parish, and his boundless energy for Christ never ceases to see needs to be met. In this excellent treatise of some of God's true champions, he paints a portrait of each one cited based on a divine virtue of Christ himself. This book will inspire, enlighten, and create a hunger for the reader to live and lead a Christ-inspired life.

David M. Griffis, D.D.
General Director
Church of God World Missions,
Cleveland, Tennessee

Just when you think the final word has been written about leadership, Bishop Ronnie Hepperly writes one that breaks the mold. He has, through personal circumstances, met these leaders. The parallels he draws between these unsung heroes and the leadership traits that have direct correlation to Biblical teaching is brilliant. What an incredible joy it is to know that God so often uses ordinary people to do extraordinary things for Him. This is a good read for anyone wishing to be used by God for Kingdom service.

Dr. R. Lamar Vest
Former General Overseer
Church of God, Cleveland, Tennessee

Reverend Ronnie Hepperly fulfills Acts 1:8: He is a Gospel witness and leader to his Judea, Samaria, and the uttermost parts of the earth. He knows how to fulfill the Biblical mandate of being a leader who reaches the lost and lifts the found. This book is special; it is not theory, but it is powerfully practical. *Passport to Leadership* will challenge and help you lead more effectively.

Dr. Raymond F. Culpepper
First Assistant General Overseer
Church of God, Cleveland, Tennessee

Bishop Ronnie Hepperly is imminently qualified to author this treatise on Christian leadership. For over thirty years, I have had the privilege to watch Bishop Hepperly's ministry grow and develop. I have known him as a friend, colleague in ministry, and even student in college classes I have taught. As both a pastor and a missionary, he lives out the qualities he brings to light in this book. Three of the ten individuals highlighted are men I have been graced to know. I very heartily agree with the insights Bishop Hepperly has gleaned from their lives. I highly recommend this book for any person who desires a deeper understanding of Christian leadership!

Raymond D. Hodge, D.Min.
Director of Business and Records
Church of God, Cleveland, Tennessee

When I think of the scripture in Genesis 6:4 which declares, "There were giants in the earth in those days," I think of Pastor Ronnie Hepperly. He is a giant in every sense of the word! Pastor Hepperly's writings are influential to those who glean from them. Only eternity will reveal the tremendous impact to those who read *Passport to Leadership*.

T. Wayne Dority
Administrative Bishop
Church of God, Cleveland, Tennessee

Passport to Leadership is a home run! It is written in an easy-to-read style that will capture the reader from the very first page. This book is filled with champions for Christ who have put their lives on the line. I highly recommend this book to all who are seeking a better understanding of what it means to be a real leader.

Dr. Ron Phillips, Pastor Emeritus
Abba's House
Hixson, Tennessee

This book is a must-read for those interested in gaining leadership training from the trenches. The author's choice to bridge the gap between contemporary leadership and those heroic Biblical leaders from the past will prove for the reader to be a very wise and relevant decision.

Dr. Darrell Bewley
Ministries Coordinator
Church of God, Cleveland, Tennessee

I have known Bishop Ronnie Hepperly for many years, observing firsthand his amazing effectiveness as a church planter, pastor, and global missionary. As this volume plumbs the traits he has discerned in extraordinary leaders—often in precarious contexts—it unself-consciously draws on Pastor Ronnie's own bold leadership intuition and ability. This book brims over with priceless Biblical and practical insights with real-life experiences. I anticipate that it will not only instruct but, more importantly, inspire readers. Highly recommended!

Tony Richie, D.Min., Ph.D.
Lead Pastor at New Harvest Church of God
Chattanooga, Tennessee

Bishop Ronnie Hepperly has used his many years of experience as a church leader and poured his heart into Passport to Leadership. This work is precise and to the point. I highly recommend it to be used as a practical tool for leadership development and ministry.

Andrew Binda, Field Director Asia/Pacific
Church of God World Missions
Cleveland, TN 37320

Occasionally in life one is privileged to encounter servants of God "of whom the world [is] not worthy." In Passport to Leadership: 10 Defining Traits and the Leaders Who Lived Them Bishop Ronnie Hepperly introduces us to women and men who are unashamedly committed to the gospel of Jesus Christ and unreservedly devoted to carry His heart and hands to those in need. This is a MUST READ! In a day when the landscape of leadership is filled with those seeking titles, here are people, ordinary people, who "out of weakness [are] made strong".

Mark L. Williams, Lead Pastor
North Cleveland Church of God
Cleveland, TN 37311

DEDICATION

I want to dedicate *Passport to Leadership* to the people who have been my best supporters and partners in this grand adventure of following Jesus around the planet.

First and foremost is my wife, Jeannie. She has always been a trooper and, quite frankly, deserves a crown! I tell everyone her greatest attribute is the ability to be a survivor. Financial and personal gain has never been the motivating factor for where we have served or lived. We have always tried to follow wherever the Lord has led and opened doors. Sometimes that has been tough on Jeannie and my boys, Bryan and Hank, but they all have been extremely supportive. So, I love you and thank you for all you have done to support me!

The ministry I have led for the last twenty years and the leadership team has been incredible. My vice president Christi Prater is a remarkable leader, pastor, educator, mother, and wife. It's hard to believe I have been blessed enough to have
some of these great leaders placed around me.

ACKNOWLEDGMENTS

Raymond Goodman: Raymond serves as my executive pastor and minister of whatever else that needs to be done. Thank you so much for your unquestioned loyalty, and your untiring effort to make the "boat float." You are a blessing, not only to RIO, but to the body of Christ. We could not do it without you!

All our unbelievable pastors, partners, donors, and members around the world: We are a team—a family—and you are special. Thank you for your partnership as we seek to follow God's will for ministry that has been entrusted to us.

Jack Niedermayer, pastor of Life Springs Church, Dunellon, Florida: I want to say what a blessing you have been! Our many conversations, along with our brainstorming sessions as we traveled the globe, and your valuable advice and technical assistance have been indispensable.

My tribe, the Church of God, Cleveland: You have helped shape this book and my ministry. Thank you for making a place for me! I am appreciative of the three ministries that have partnered with me to accomplish this project: David Ray at Pathway Press, and the Church of God Publishing House; Mitch Maloney and USA Missions; and David Griffis and Church of God World Missions. I really love you all—thanks again!

Dr. J. Tod Zeiger: Last, but not least, thank you Dr. Zeiger! I honor and respect you. Without your experience and assistance, this project would never have happened. I'm looking forward to many years of fruitful partnership as we seek to raise up, reproduce, and release disciples!

CONTENTS

FOREWORD
INTRODUCTION

CONCLUSION

FOREWORD

It has been said that leadership is not about a title or a designation, but about impact, influence, and inspiration. The leaders described in *Passport to Leadership* were (and are) impactful, influential, and truly inspirational. The traits of each of these leaders provide us with a roadmap for our own leadership paths. We must continue to learn and hone our skills—never satisfied that we have achieved our highest level. A leader is responsible to help others reach their greatest potential, but that begins within the leader himself.

One great leader is missing in this book and that is the author, Bishop Ronnie Hepperly. Bishop Hepperly is an inspirational leader. He is able to effectively inspire teams of people to execute a plan of action and achieve great results. He is known as one who shares the successes with his team, celebrating what God has done. This is a trait of a great leader. This is a trait of Bishop Ronnie Hepperly.

May each leader who reads this book apply these lessons to become his or her best. As Proverbs 27:17 states, "Iron sharpens iron, so one person sharpens another" (NIV).

M. Thomas Propes, D.D.
Assistant Director of World Missions
Church of God, Cleveland, Tennessee

INTRODUCTION

My goal in writing this book on leadership is not so much about telling "how it's done," as it is what do real-life unsung heroes look like. Each chapter of this book is a description of ordinary people who rose to the level of the extraordinary. They defined *leadership* as putting one foot in front of the other, all the while trusting God and pressing forward. These sacrificial servants are people I know personally and have labored beside them year in and year out. I have witnessed up close and personal the sacrifice and dedication of each leader. Some that I will be writing about have already received their reward and are part of the "great cloud of witnesses" of Hebrews 12.

My aim in sharing their stories is to let the reader know that their influence lives on in the pages of this book, and in the lives of the people they mentored, ministered to, and influenced. Many of the people I've written about are fathers, mothers, and quite a few are even grandparents in the later chapters of the book of their lives. They, like me, want to finish strong and desperately want to leave a legacy.

Most of the people described in this book will deny the fact they are heroes. Obviously, I would adamantly disagree! Just because some are poor (by Western standards) or uneducated is not a reason to be disqualified from demonstrating extraordinary qualities of leadership. Some of the subjects in this book have never owned an automobile or their own home. They are more familiar with thatch roofs and dirt floors than they are with the amenities of the modern society. Be that as it may, these people are all my family by choice. No, they are not blood relatives, but they are all my family and feel the same about me. Only one of these incredible leaders came from a wealthy family, and only one was highly educated. Neither of them has allowed those designations to determine who they are or who they minister to.

As a man working primarily with other men has limited my interaction with the opposite gender. But, the one lady that I write about does not need to take a backseat to anyone. Her ability to lead under pressure is well-documented and celebrated.

All but one of my stories are about people who are, or have been, in full-time vocational ministry. The very first story in the book is about a man who worked in a factory most of his life. This giant of the faith influenced me and many others of my generation either directly or indirectly. I dare say his influence on my life was much more than most teachers, pastors, denominational leaders, politicians, and governmental authorities.

Leadership heroes come in all shapes, sizes, genders, races, and nationalities! First Corinthians 1:27-29 declares: "But God has chosen the foolish things of the world to put to shame the wise, and God has chosen the weak things of the world to put to shame the things which are mighty; and the base things of the world and the things which are despised God has chosen, and the things which are not, to bring to nothing the things that are, that no flesh should glory in His presence" (NKJV).

My intention is not to give you an exhaustive list of leadership traits. I aim to showcase some incredibly essential characteristics that have enabled average, everyday people, to achieve greatness in their areas of service. My target audience is first and foremost people who may be living ordinary lives who seek to make a difference by using their God-given talents and abilities. I realize the academic and the non-Christian may choose to pass this book by for those very reasons. But my purpose must be plain and straightforward. I have no question whatsoever this book could bless a highly educated person, and there is no doubt in my mind that a non-Christian could improve their leadership skills by learning some of the characteristics that are described in these pages.

Finally, let me reiterate my primary goal is to bring focus to some very special people who are, or have been, on the front lines of battle doing extraordinary exploits for the kingdom of God. The things they have done, or are doing, have become the passport to their leadership journeys. My prayer is that we all will continue to grow in our ability to lead others and leave a legacy as we seek to follow and serve the Lord Jesus Christ!

AUTHOR'S NOTE

At the beginning of each chapter, there is a personal story that relates to a true-life person that I have had the privilege of working with and observing up close and personal. Each person mentioned is a personification of leadership traits that have a direct correlation to Biblical teaching that I share in the latter part of each chapter. I am by no means suggesting that these men and women were flawless, or were the only ones who demonstrated such traits. I chose them to represent a microcosm of a larger picture of committed believers to the cause of Christ. I pray God's blessings on you as you read the following chapters.

Chapter 1

DEDICATION

James "Nero" Dockery

And whatsoever ye do in word or deed, do all in the name of the Lord Jesus, giving thanks to God and the Father by him (Colossians 3:17).

When I think about the word *dedication,* my thoughts turn toward a man who was my mentor and friend. His name was James "Nero" Dockery. I have often thought if you looked up the word *dedication* in the dictionary, you might find his picture next to the word. The definition of the word *dedication* is "the quality of being dedicated or committed to a task or purpose." And, some of the most popular synonyms are *commitment, wholeheartedness, single-mindedness, enthusiasm, and zeal.*[1] The dictionary's definition of *dedication* is a perfect description of the man I came to know and love as my mentor, my fellow soldier in the Gospel, and my friend.

According to the world's standards (and the modern church), he would not even register on the "hero scale." After all, he didn't pastor a large church or any church for that matter. He wasn't considered wealthy, or a man of political clout. No, he was a working man, who took care of his family. His love of the outdoors was only outweighed by his love to sing about Jesus. This "everyman" made sure those around him knew they could count on him. That's what dedication looked like; when the going got tough, he strapped on his big-boy boots and headed toward the battle!

To be clear, challenge and sacrifice were definitely not uncommon in Nero's world.

I was just a kid when I met James. To say he made an impact on my life would be an understatement. He was one of the respected men in the church. Time after time this man gave of himself to mentor and guide, not only me but many men. He helped us navigate through the potholes and ditches along the leadership highway; and believe me, it wasn't easy.

I dare say, more than any other leader his influence was felt in the formation of the RIO Network. There are at least four men who are now pastoring in RIO churches that could testify how this man made a difference in their lives. No hour was too late, and no subject was off limits. For instance, one day I asked him about tithing. I wanted to know how he felt about it, so I said, "Brother James, what do you think about tithing?" You know what he did? He didn't sit me down and preach to me with a Bible pushed in my face. No, he handed me a folded piece of paper with Scripture verses about tithing. The implication was, "Here's what the Bible says about it, so go and seek the Lord for yourself!" By the way, I still have that piece of paper today, and it means more to me than you can imagine.

The Lord called James home at the young age of 64. I was blessed to be able to share with him the night before he died. I will always treasure those moments because, as with all of us, we do not know what tomorrow may bring. He stepped into eternity the next morning, but he left a lasting legacy for us to emulate!

As far as personal stories, they are too many to mention here. But, I will share one that illustrates my point of a dedicated man. A situation happened after the Lord

18

called Nero home. One cold, wet Sunday morning, when I arrived at church, I discovered there was NO heat in the building. To be honest, we just took for granted that Nero would take it on himself to make sure things like that were handled. After all, he was the "go-to" man, the "fix-it" guy. He was always there early on Sunday morning to make sure everything was right. If you needed something done, well, go to the man who would take responsibility to see it through. On this cold Sunday morning, he was enjoying the warm fellowship of the Lord, and we were facing church without heat.

So, here I am stressed and aggravated to the max, wondering what to do. I got another man to help me, Jay Bryant, and we climbed a ladder and removed tiles out of the dropped ceiling. We had to find and relight the furnaces. I'm sure we looked a sight all dressed up in our suits and ties, trying to figure out how not to get filthy and still get the job done. To say we were unprepared is an understatement. We had good intentions, but no matches. The last time I checked, good intentions won't keep you warm on a cold winter day!

Much to our delight, Nero had already prepared for such an emergency. We found matches in waterproof containers alongside all the furnaces. In short order, the crises were averted because one dedicated man made sure we would never be without heat! I went from being mad and upset to being thankful for a man of dedication who knew how to get the job done.

James "Nero" Dockery was proof you don't have to stand behind a pulpit or live your life hiding behind the four walls of a church to leave a legacy of spiritual treasure. No, he demonstrated dedication to his church, his family, and in the lives of others because of his supreme commitment to the Lord Jesus Christ. My prayer is the Lord will give us more men and women of dedication who don't have to have the spotlight or the applause of the crowd. These unsung heroes of the faith who stand firmly dedicated to the Lord Jesus Christ are the ones who are making a difference.

What does dedication look like? Why is it essential to the kingdom of God? Jesus said in Matthew 6:33, "But seek first the kingdom of God and His righteousness, and all these things shall be added to you" (NKJV). If that be true, and it is, then why aren't we seeing more men and women dedicated to the gospel of the Kingdom?

Go ahead, look up the word *dedication*, and you just might see his picture!

***

There are many examples of dedication in the Bible. The list is long, but I have to say there is one that stands out more than the rest. His name is Nehemiah. He was dedicated to the task of rebuilding the walls around Jerusalem, and he did so at a massive personal cost.

I find many parallels between my mentor, James Dockery, and this man Nehemiah. Both men were considered "can-do" guys. Both men, when confronted with a need, didn't just talk a good game, they took action.

Let's consider a few things about Nehemiah and see how his dedication led to a revival of a distressed and discouraged nation. His dedication is outlined in the book named after him. Let's take a brief glimpse at his "Memoirs" and learn what made this "Spirit-filled building contractor" do the things that he did. Time and space won't allow for a detailed examination of his exploits, but we can glean some nuggets of gold that will help us to become better leaders.

1. He Was a Common Man

Nehemiah 1:1-4

The words of Nehemiah the son of Hachaliah. And it came to pass in the month Chisleu, in the twentieth year, as I was in Shushan the palace, that Hanani, one of my brethren, came, he and certain men of Judah; and I asked them concerning the Jews that had escaped, which were left of the captivity, and concerning Jerusalem. And they said unto me, The remnant that are left of the captivity there in the province are in great affliction and reproach: the wall of Jerusalem also is broken down, and the gates thereof are burned with fire. And it came to pass, when I heard these words, that I sat down and wept, and mourned certain days, and fasted, and prayed before the God of heaven.

His "day job" was one that not many people would aspire to or hope to get one day. He was a cupbearer to the most powerful man on the planet, King Artaxerxes, the king of Persia (2:1-3). If you were the cupbearer to the king, it was your job to "taste-test" everything before the king could put his royal lips to whatever was being served. If an enemy tried to poison the king, the cupbearer would be the first to hit the floor.

Nehemiah was not a prophet, priest, or king. He was, in my humble estimation, an ordinary working man who was called on by God to do an extraordinary thing. He lived as a slave, in a foreign country, and yet that did not

21

stop him from becoming a man that God could use to do great things. The heroes of the faith are men like James Dockery, Nehemiah, and a long list of people who would not be considered great, except in the hallowed hall of heaven!

Before you give up on your dream of being used by God because you feel "stuck" on the shelf, remember:

- Moses was tending sheep on the backside of the desert when God showed up and renewed his calling as the deliverer of the Hebrew nation.

- It was a man named Gideon who was hiding from the enemy when God spoke to his future.

- It was a teenager named David who dared take on Goliath, all the while the trained soldiers of Saul were hiding in fear.

- It was a poor teenage girl by the name of Esther who was elevated to the queen of a nation to save the Jewish people.

- It was a persecutor of the Church named Saul, who later became Paul, who shook two continents for Christ.

The Apostle Paul put it this way in 1 Corinthians 1:25-29: "Because the foolishness of God is wiser than men; and the weakness of God is stronger than men. For ye see your calling, brethren, how that not many wise men after the flesh, not many mighty, not many noble, are called: But God hath chosen the foolish things of the world to confound the wise; and God hath chosen the weak things of the world to confound the things which are mighty; and base things of the world, and things which are despised, hath God chosen, yea, and things which are not, to bring to nought things that are: that no flesh should glory in his presence."

Yes, God has used and will use again ordinary people to accomplish extraordinary things, all because they are dedicated to the gospel of Christ.

2. He Was a Concerned Man

When Nehemiah heard the report from his brothers, he was deeply distressed: "And it came to pass, when I heard these words, that I sat down and wept, and mourned certain days, and fasted, and prayed before the God of heaven" (1:4). The wall around the city lay in ruins and the gates were burned, and something had to be done about that!

His concern led him to fast, pray, and eventually share with the king what needed to be done. Do you see a pattern here? He wasn't the kind of man who saw a need and refused to get his hands dirty. James 2:16 says, "And one of you say unto them, Depart in peace, be ye warmed and filled; notwithstanding ye give them not those things which are needful to the body; what doth it profit?" James is reflecting the typical attitude of those who think that because you talk about a need, the need will be met.

Nehemiah, James Dockery, and many others were the kind of men that God could use. Why? Their genuine concern and dedication to the fulfillment of a task will always stand "head and shoulders" above those who just show up to be seen. In the days we are living in, it is no longer acceptable to play church and fake concern for others. People are dying without Christ, the walls of protection are down, and the gates of entry are burned and left wide open for the enemy to do his dirty work.

Cyril J. Barber, in his excellent book, *Nehemiah and the Dynamics of Effective Leadership,* wrote:

> *All too often a would-be leader tries to climb the ladder of success by treading on others. He exploits their abilities to secure his own advancement. The importance of the vital regard for others has been stressed by Sir Arthur Bryant. In an article published in the* Illustrated London News, *this renowned historian said: "No one is fit to lead his fellows unless he holds their care and well-being to be his prime responsibility, his duty . . . his privilege."*

> Barber continued: *A wise leader places the welfare of those with whom he worked high on his priority list. He ensures that their concerns are taken care of ahead of his own. He knows that if they are relatively free from personal anxiety, they can perform better on the job. No business corporation or church, educational institution or mission, can succeed in achieving a goal without the willing assistance of those who are prepared to give of themselves for the sake of the work.*[2]

3. He Was a Criticized Man

It was only after Nehemiah began rebuilding the wall that the critics showed up: "But it came to pass, that when Sanballat heard that we builded the wall, he was wroth, and took great indignation, and mocked the Jews. And he spake before his brethren and the army of

Samaria, and said, What do these feeble Jews? will they fortify themselves? will they sacrifice? will they make an end in a day? will they revive the stones out of the heaps of the rubbish which are burned? Now Tobiah the Ammonite was by him, and he said, Even that which they build, if a fox go up, he shall even break down their stone wall" (Nehemiah 4:1-3).

Nehemiah's enemies started with sarcasm, continued with mockery, and piled on with criticism. And before it was over, the enemy even tried to kill him! (see chapter 6).

My mentor and friend taught me many leadership lessons. But, the most valuable thing he did was live a godly life and be an example of dedication in his everyday walk. He always pushed through any and all opposition and persevered.

You don't have to look very far in the Book of Nehemiah to discover the ones who fueled the opposition were the ones who were on the outside looking in. Their only purpose in life was to stop God's work. You notice that every time Nehemiah was criticized he never stopped the work to argue, haggle, or justify what he was doing. It seemed the more bricks of accusation that were thrown at him, he picked them up and kept building the wall!

The next time you are feeling down and discouraged, remember that the greatest leader who ever lived was criticized. His name was Jesus Christ. In Matthew 11:19, He was called a glutton and a drunk. In Matthew 9:11, He was criticized for hanging out with the wrong crowd. And, believe it or not, in John 8:48, He was accused of having a demon. So, if you are facing criticism, cheer up, you are in good company!

4. He Was a Courageous Man

Do you know what Nehemiah did when he was opposed? He kept going, and as far as I can see, he never even complained. He didn't stop the work just because there were those who didn't like it. "So built we the wall; and all the wall was joined together unto the half thereof: for the people had a mind to work" (Nehemiah 4:6). Nehemiah and the people had a mind to work, a heart to pray, and a dedication to see the job through.

As we look at 6:1-2, we see . . . "Now it came to pass when Sanballat, and Tobiah, and Geshem the Arabian, and the rest of our enemies, heard that I had builded the wall, and that there was no breach left therein; (though at that time I had not set up the doors upon the gates;) that Sanballat and Geshem sent unto me, saying, Come, let us meet together in some one of the villages in the plain of Ono. But they thought to do me mischief."

I can only speculate what might have happened to the work had Nehemiah lost his dedication and courage to finish the job. One thing is sure, and that is no great work has ever been accomplished without passion, dedication, and courage. It would have been easy for him to bend to the wishes of the "noisy critics" and move on back to his cushy job serving the king. Thank God he had a stiff spine and bold spirit that would not let him quit until the wall was rebuilt.

Recently I read an article titled "Are Courageous Christians a Thing of the Past?" Author Don Schanzenbach observed:

> *In every age people are challenged. They are forced to make choices that will affect their families*

and nations for generations into the future. The need for men and women of uncommon courage, dedication, perseverance, and self-sacrifice recurs over the centuries. As we read about the mighty deeds done in past eras we are inspired to imitate the heroic behavior of those brave hearts who went before. Christian culture has been threatened many times. Now, when our faith is often mocked and the churches seem unwilling to pursue any courageous course, God is again calling His saints to sacrifice and dedication in the defense of right.[3]

Once again the devil underestimated the strength and resolve of this man who determined not to waver, but move straight ahead. After all, what could this group of ragtag people led by a former slave accomplish? Not much, except for the outstanding leadership of Nehemiah.

In recounting the heroic deeds performed by the Marines during the bloody battle of Iwo Jima that took place from February 19 to March 25, 1945, Admiral Chester W. Nimitz said: "By their victory, the 3rd, 4th and 5th Marine Divisions and other units of the Fifth Amphibious Corps have made an accounting to their country which only history will be able to value fully. *Among the Americans serving on Iwo island, uncommon valor was a common virtue.*"[4]

Much like those Marines on Iwo Jima, God has given us men and women who are still displaying an uncommon courage in the face of a determined enemy. Through the years I have had the privilege of working with many people. I have observed up close and personal some of the qualities that make a great leader. If I had to write a single statement that defined James Dockery as it relates to the example of Nehemiah, I would sincerely say: *He finished the wall!*

29

DISCUSSION QUESTIONS

1. When you consider the word *dedication* and *commitment,* who is the first person that comes to mind?

2. Describe (in detail) and share how this person has made an impact on your life.

3. Why do you think Nehemiah refused to stop building the wall and discuss the situation with his detractors?

4. In your estimation, is there a lack of dedication and commitment as it relates to the kingdom of God?

5. What challenges are you facing today that would impact your dedication to the kingdom of God? Job? Lack of time? Lack of resources?

NOTES

1. Definition of *dedication: https://en.oxforddictionaries.com/definition/dedication* (accessed September 20, 2018).

2. Cyril J. Barber, *Nehemiah and the Dynamics of Effective Leadership* (Neptune, NJ: Loizeaux Brothers, 1976) 25-26.

3. Don Schanzenbach, "Are Courageous Christians a Thing of the Past?" *http://www.missiontorestoreamerica.com/blog/courageous-christians/* (accessed September 24, 2018).

4. Chester W. Nimitz's statement after the Battle of Iwo Jima (c. March-May, 1945); "UNCOMMON VALOR WAS A COMMON VIRTUE" has been inscribed on the *USMC War Memorial. https://en.wikiquote.org/wiki/Chester_W._Nimitz* (accessed September 25, 2018).

Chapter 2

HUMILITY

Elias Garcia

But he giveth more grace. Wherefore he saith, God resisteth the proud, but giveth grace unto the humble. Submit yourselves therefore to God. Resist the devil, and he will flee from you. Draw nigh to God, and he will draw nigh to you. Cleanse your hands, ye sinners; and purify your hearts, ye double minded. Be afflicted, and mourn, and weep: let your laughter be turned to mourning, and your joy to heaviness. Humble yourselves in the sight of the Lord, and he shall lift you up (James 4:6-10).

The country of Panama is known for many things, not the least of which is the relationship this beautiful country has shared with the United States over the past one hundred plus years. Remember, it was the saga of one of the most infamous men who ever occupied the president's office in Panama City that captured our attention in the late eighties and early nineties. His name was Manuel Noriega. In 1992, Noriega was convicted and sentenced to forty years in prison for drug trafficking and money laundering. Little did I know that one day our lives would intersect and I would have the opportunity to go to his prison and pray for him!

My relationship with Panama began a few years before my encounter with Noriega. In 2000 I made my trip to this beautiful country, and it was love at first sight! Since that first trip, I have made approximately ninety-nine more.

That should tell you all you need to know about how I feel about this special place with its rich history, beautiful landscapes, and its hardworking people. The precious believers in Panama know the meaning of hardships and, in spite of the obstacles, continue to spread the saving message of Jesus Christ.

It was during one of those early trips that I met a man who forever impacted my life. His name is Elias Garcia. When I think of the attitude of *humility,* his face comes to mind. His life is the essence of the definition. Elias lives in the mountains of the central part of Panama with his wife and five children. Unless you have been there, it is hard to imagine how difficult it must be to work and support a family under such difficult conditions.

According to Merriam-Webster, *humility* means "the state of being humble." Both it and *humble* have their origin in the Latin word *humilis,* meaning "low."[1] In his attitude and actions, I found Elias to be a man who lives out the message of the One who was the very incarnation of humility, the Lord Jesus Christ.

The Apostle Paul, in referring to Jesus, said, "Who, being in the form of God, thought it not robbery to be equal with God: but made himself of no reputation, and took upon him the form of a servant, and was made in the likeness of men: And being found in fashion as a man, he *humbled himself,* and became obedient unto death, even the death of the cross" (Philippians 2:6-8).

One of the most glaring leadership traits today is the polar opposite of humility. I am referring to pride and self-promotion. Sadly, many ego- driven leaders think the whole world revolves around them. The attitude of self-promotion and pride didn't start in our generation. The Lord Jesus had to deal with the issue of pride and self-promotion among His disciples.

Matthew 18:1-4 tells us: "At the same time came the disciples unto Jesus, saying, Who is the greatest in the kingdom of heaven? And Jesus called a little child unto him, and set him in the midst of them, and said, Verily I say unto you, Except ye be converted, and become as little children, ye shall not enter into the kingdom of heaven. Whosoever therefore shall humble himself as this little child, the same is greatest in the kingdom of heaven."

Again, in 23:11-13 He said, "But he who is greatest among you shall be your servant. And whoever exalts himself will be humbled, and he who humbles himself will be exalted. But woe to you, scribes and Pharisees, hypocrites! For you shut up the kingdom of heaven against men; for you neither go in yourselves, nor do you allow those who are entering to go in."

Pastor Eston Williams observed:

Jesus' suggestion that the essence of greatness is humility is not an idea that is easily sold in this day and age. Humility and meekness are not what you would call sexy character traits. Can you imagine Madison Avenue selecting a humble person to be the spokesperson for a new car? Who would be attracted to that? Our culture worships success, power, ambition, fame and wealth. Just wouldn't make sense to see Mother Teresa hawking deodorant, would it? William Bennet edited an enormous tome a few years ago called The Book of Virtues. *In it he listed a vast array of virtues such as self-discipline, responsibility, work, perseverance, loyalty, courage, faith, honesty, compassion and friendship. Humility did not make the list. Do we look for humility in our leaders? Do we list humility as a character trait on our resumes? If you claimed to be humble, would you be bragging?*[2]

To my way of thinking, the ability to humble yourself may be the most important of all leadership traits. I have worked with leaders from around the world, and it is not always the most popular or the most educated that get the job done. It is the unsung heroes who walk, work, and witness with a humble spirit. It was author John Ruskin who said, "I believe the first test of a truly great man is his humility,"[3] to which I say AMEN!

The Bible has much to say about the attitude of *humility*. Below is a brief sampling. (The following references are from the *New King James Version*).

Proverbs 3:34: "Surely He scorns the scornful, but gives grace to the humble."

Proverbs 11:2: "When pride comes, then comes shame; but with the humble is wisdom."

Philippians 2:1-4: "Therefore if there is any consolation in Christ, if any comfort of love, if any fellowship of the Spirit, if any affection and mercy, fulfill my joy by being like-minded, having the same love, being of one accord, of one mind. Let nothing be done through selfish ambition or conceit, but in lowliness of mind let each esteem others better than himself. Let each of you look out not only for his own interests, but also for the interests of others."

Colossians 3:12: "Therefore, as the elect of God, holy and beloved, put on tender mercies, kindness, humility, meekness, longsuffering."

1 Peter 5:5: "Likewise you younger people, submit yourselves to your elders. Yes, all of you be submissive to one another, and be clothed with humility, for 'God resists the proud, but gives grace to the humble.'"

In his book titled *HUMILITY,* Andrew Murray wrote: *How to conquer pride:* "Two things are needed. Do what God says is your work—humble yourself. Trust Him to do what He says is His work; He will exalt you."[4]

***

During those early days, Elias and I formed a bond that has grown stronger every year. I spent many hours with Elias and his precious family. I watched him labor under very intense circumstances. I have never heard one word of complaint, not one. I am not suggesting Elias is perfect, but his humble attitude and selfless spirit is what is so attractive about his life and ministry.

In many ways, my relationship with Elias mirrored that of Paul and Timothy. Paul loved Timothy as his own son, just as I love Elias and his family as my very own. I have never been around him that I didn't see the attitude of a humble man, who is willing to go the extra mile to share the gospel of Christ.

The Apostle Paul wrote two letters to his young protégé in the ministry. We can glean a treasure trove of insight just by looking at three things:

Consider:

1. Timothy Was a SON

To Timothy, my dearly beloved son: Grace, mercy, and peace, from God the Father and Christ Jesus our Lord (2 Timothy 1:2).

The relationship that Paul had with Timothy was spiritual. Since Paul was not his earthly father, how could he call him his "dearly beloved son"? We are told Timothy was raised in a religious home, the product of a mixed marriage. His mother was Jewish, and his father was Greek (see 2 Timothy 1:5). When Paul and his team arrived in Timothy's hometown, the brethren spoke to Paul about a young man who had a good reputation. Many believe it was Paul who led this young man to Christ and took him under his wing. Timothy joined the missionary team and became a vital part of the ministry. Therefore, Timothy became Paul's spiritual son in the faith (see Acts 16:1-2).

The relationship that Paul had with Timothy was special. At some point, Timothy was assigned the task of pastoring the church at Ephesus. All you have to do is read the two letters that Paul wrote to discover some of the issues Timothy faced.

This young pastor faced many of the difficulties that we can all relate too. He had physical issues (see 1 Timothy 5:23), and at times found himself in the pit of discouragement. Apparently, there were some in the Church who criticized him for being too young to carry such a heavy responsibility (see 1 Timothy 4:12). It is no wonder that Paul had to encourage him to "make full proof of [his] ministry" (2 Timothy 4:5). In practical language, he was telling Timothy it was too soon to quit and go home! I think we can all relate, don't you? The Lord only knows how many times we have heard that criticism and so much more!

I am convinced every Paul needs a Timothy and every Timothy needs a Paul. Having a Paul in your life is having someone who has been on the trail a lot longer than you have. A mentor, guide, and trusted friend is essential to keep us from falling into the "ruts, potholes, and ditches" of ministry.

Likewise, every Paul needs a Timothy. I have several young Timothys that look to me for counsel (when needed) and advice on a wide range of ministry issues. I learned a long time ago that asking someone for counsel doesn't mean you are ignorant; it just says you haven't found the right answer yet! Proverbs 27:17 tells us, "Iron sharpeneth iron; so a man sharpeneth the countenance of his friend." I must confess having Timothys around keeps my blade sharp.

Of course, I consider Elias Garcia as one of my Timothys in the faith. No, I am not his earthly father, but our relationship is both *spiritual* and *special.* It has been my joy to watch him grow in faith, and stretch the boundaries of his influence. We all need someone to look to for direction and wisdom. The distance between us may be over 3,000 miles, but when God puts someone in your life, the number of miles is irrelevant.

2. Timothy Was a SERVANT

And the servant of the Lord must not strive; but be gentle unto all men, apt to teach, patient, in meekness instructing those that oppose themselves; if God peradventure will give them repentance to the

38

acknowledging of the truth; and that they may recover themselves out of the snare of the devil, who are taken captive by him at his will (2 Timothy 2:24-26).

He was a faithful servant. In spite of his limitations, Paul knew he could trust young Timothy with the assignment of leading the church in Ephesus. Paul spent nearly three years in that city, and he knew it was going to be a challenging assignment (see Acts 19). Here was a young preacher thrust into a city that was given over to the worship of Diana, the queen of sexual immorality. Timothy faced opposition from without and from within and yet stayed the course.

When I first met Elias, he was serving in the local church. At some point, the pastor of the church left without warning. The church needed a shepherd, so our network brought the church under our covering and appointed Elias as pastor.

Similarly, Elias, like Timothy, was given the challenging assignment of leading a local church and was willing to do whatever it took to reach people for Christ.

He was a fearless servant. When Timothy needed encouragement, Paul did not baby or coddle him. I don't care how long one has been in ministry, there may come a time when fear will stalk and harass us. Paul's word to Timothy (and to us) was, "For God hath not given us the spirit of fear; but of power, and of love, and of a sound mind" (2 Timothy 1:7). *Vines Greek New Testament Dictionary* defines the word *fear* as used in 2 Timothy 1:7 as "cowardice and timidity and is never used in a good sense."[5] It comes with the idea of running away from a fight!

Running away from the heat of battle was foreign to Paul's vocabulary. Down to the very end of his life, he could say, "For I am now ready to be offered, and the time of my departure is at hand. I have fought a good fight, I have finished my course, I have kept the faith" (2 Timothy 4:6-7). The next time the devil launches a missile of fear at your heart, remember you have three spiritual qualities that will blow it up before it ever hits the target. It is the Holy Spirit that gives us the enablement to serve, witness, and walk without fear and timidity.

Look at what we have:

*We have the *power (dunamis)* of God to face and overcome any circumstance. The same word for "power" is used in Acts 1:8: "But ye shall receive power, after that the Holy Ghost is come upon you: and ye shall be witnesses unto me both in Jerusalem, and in all Judaea, and in Samaria, and unto the uttermost part of the earth."

*We have the *love (agape)* of God to endure any hardship in order to win lost souls to Christ. According to Galatians 5:22-23, *agape* love is a product of the indwelling Holy Spirit: "But the fruit of the Spirit is love, joy, peace, longsuffering, gentleness, goodness, faith, meekness, temperance: against such there is no law." Preferring others above our own needs may be the greatest test of a humble spirit.

*We have a *sound mind* to live a disciplined life. The phrase "sound mind" could be better translated, "sober-minded" or "self-disciplined." The Holy Spirit gives us the ability to live a "calm and self-controlled" life. Titus 2:12 tells us, "Teaching us that, denying ungodliness and worldly lusts, we should live soberly, righteously, and godly, in this present world."

Paul's word may have been directed toward Timothy, but all ministers of the Gospel need to understand the same truth; without the power of the Holy Spirit, we are helpless to paralyzing fear that is designed to drive us away from reaching lost souls for Christ.

Elias, like Timothy, was fearless in the face of any roadblock that might hinder the Gospel. We traveled to some of the most remote and dangerous places in Panama to plant churches and share the good news with pastors and people. We purchased eight horses to ride because some of the locations were too difficult even for four-wheeled vehicles to travel. We gave Elias two for his ministry. He was like the Pony Express: he would ride one till it gave out, and grab the other one and keep going. He might have been small in stature; but make no mistake, he was ten feet tall in the things of God!

This *fearless servant* was not afraid to get his hands dirty. It seemed every time I would go back to Panama to minister, he would show me some new project he completed on one of our churches. He was willing to do whatever was required. Whether it was leading a service, sweeping the floor, or laying block for a new building, his response was always the same . . . YES!

3. Timothy Was a SOLDIER

Thou therefore endure hardness, as a good soldier of Jesus Christ. No man that warreth entangleth himself with the affairs of this life; that he may please him who hath chosen him to be a soldier (2 Timothy 2:3-4).

As a soldier, there are things to endure. The phrase "endure hardness" means to "bear evil treatment." If you have been in ministry for very long, you know that being a preacher of the Gospel carries its own unique challenges. Whether we want to admit it or not, we are in a war (see Ephesians 6:10-12). In Paul's day, some who were once involved were now wanting to retreat from battle (see 2 Timothy 4:10). Reaching others with the Good News is a battleground to endure, not a playground to enjoy.

"Men of prayer must be men of steel, for they will be assaulted by Satan even before they attempt to assault his kingdom."—Leonard Ravenhill[6]

I can still remember one of our earliest trips. The location was remote, and when I say "remote," I mean miles and miles from civilization! As it turned out, we didn't have enough animals for everyone. I tried to get Elias to take turns with me, so we could both ride and walk an equal amount. He wouldn't hear of it, period. In his humble way, he couldn't imagine the man of God walking while he was riding! Hour after hour I watched him with only his black rubber boots for protection, as he slogged through swamps, rivers, and over some of the roughest ground you could imagine.

As a soldier, there are things to avoid. Paul is speaking of a professional soldier, one who is totally committed to his commander: "No man that warreth entangleth himself with the affairs of this life." He is not saying to disengage from the world, or move to a mountaintop and meditate twenty-four hours a day. He said we must not be so "intertwined" with the things of the world that we lose focus on the eternal issues of life.

As a soldier, there are things to gain. As a Christian, our purpose is to "please him who hath chosen him to be a soldier." That's it—nothing more, nothing less than to hear our Heavenly Commander declare, "Well done, thou good and faithful servant: thou hast been faithful over a few things, I will make thee ruler over many things: enter thou into the joy of thy lord" (Matthew 25:21).

On this final thought, let there be no debate; we need, and we must have an earth-shaking revival! The secret to such an event is no secret at all. It is plainly spelled out in the Word of God. It will take men like Elias Garcia who walk in a humble spirit, who are willing to stay the course and strictly obey the command of 2 Chronicles 7:14: "If my people, which are called by my name, *shall humble* themselves, and pray, and seek my face, and turn from their wicked ways; then will I hear from heaven, and will forgive their sin, and will heal their land."

Will you be one?

DISCUSSION QUESTIONS

1. Is there a difference between *being humble* and *being humiliated*? Discuss.

2. Read 2 Chronicles 7:14 again and discuss the various ingredients to revival. For instance: To whom is the writer referring to when he says, "If my people"? What does the Scripture mean when it says, "shall humble themselves"?

3. Timothy was not Paul's son in the flesh, but in the faith. Do you have a son or daughter in the faith that considers you a mentor? If not, why not?

4. As a Christian, do you find it difficult to grasp the concept that you are a "soldier" in God's army? What does a Christian soldier look like, act like, dress like? (see Ephesians 6).

5. First Peter 5:5 says, "God resists the proud, but gives grace to the humble" (NKJV). In what way does God "resist the proud"? You must discuss Scriptures, not just opinions.

NOTES

1. Definition of *humility: https://www.merriam-webster.com/dictionary/humility* (accessed October 3, 2018).

2. Eston Williams, *Humility*, *https://www.sermoncentral.com/sermons/humility-eston-williams* (accessed October 4, 2018).

3. John Ruskin, as quoted in *Josiah Hotchkiss Gilbert's Dictionary of Burning Words of Brilliant Writers* (1895) 330. *https://en.wikiquote.org/wiki/Humility* (accessed October 8, 2018).

4. Andrew Murray, *HUMILITY: The Beauty of Holiness* (Abbotsford, WI: Life Sentence Publishing, 2016) 90.

5. Definition of *fear* as used in 2 Timothy 1:7, *Vine's Greek New Testament Dictionary, http://gospelhall.org/bible/bible.php?search=FEAR&dict=vine&lang=english* (accessed October 8, 2018).

6. Leonard Ravenhill, *Why Revival Tarries* (Zachary, LA: Fires of Revival Publishers, 1972) 77.

Chapter 3

CONFIDENCE

Millie Lumiti

Being confident of this very thing, that he which hath begun a good work in you will perform it until the day of Jesus Christ (Philippians 1:6).

Baker's Evangelical Dictionary describes *confidence* as "a multifaceted word that encompasses within Christian thought a range of aspects of faith in God, certainty and assurance of one's relationship with God, a sense of boldness that is dependent on a realization of one's acceptance by God, and a conviction that one's destiny is secure in God."[1]

Over fifteen years ago I met a woman named Millie Lumiti, who is a perfect example of the above description of the word *confidence.* I could use several words to describe her: courage; determination; persistence; boldness. But, the one word that best describes her is *confidence.*

I am not talking about a *self-confidence* that eliminates any need of God's power and provision. In her case, everything about her life exudes confidence and trust in the Lord. No matter what may come her way, she believes God will work it out for His glory and her good! Her confidence in God's plans for her life is fixed on a firm foundation of trust that she, like Paul, can declare, "*I can do all things* through Christ which strengtheneth me*" (Philippians 4:13).

When we first met, Millie Lumiti was living in Nairobi, Kenya. She had been assigned to me as my translator. I remember in those early days she would accompany me to translate while I preached in some of the toughest prisons in Africa. I watched as her heart began to break for the lost, and before long, she was consumed with a desire to reach as many with the Gospel as possible. She was much more than a translator, as she became a dynamic preacher of the Gospel. Her compassion and dedication led us to appoint her as the director of our prison ministry in Africa.

Her confidence in Christ was born out of a necessity to trust Him in spite of circumstances. She learned the same secret that the Apostle Paul spoke of in Philippians 4:12-13: "I know what it is to be in need, and I know what it is to have plenty. I have learned the secret of being content in any and every situation, whether well fed or hungry, whether living in plenty or in want. I can do all this through him who gives me strength" (NIV). I do not doubt that Millie could echo an amen to his words!

She knows that life can be unfair, unjust, and at times very cruel. The thing that blesses me is how she handles those situations. Her first reaction is to pray and trust God. Instead of fearing the future, she embraces it with the full confidence that God will always work things out.

On more than one occasion, Millie has used her own money to buy clothes, underwear, and other necessities for women prisoners. She did it even to the neglect of her own needs. She is willing to go to any lengths to see people saved, healed, and delivered.

Millie's confidence also comes from her firsthand knowledge of God's unlimited resources to fight the battle. Whatever situation may arise, the indwelling Holy Spirit has made her more than a conqueror through the One who loved her and gave Himself for her.

In a message by Pastor Ron Thomas, he asked the following questions:

Are you a confident Christian? Where is your confidence?

Biblical confidence and cultural confidence are opposed to each other. While everyone places confidence in someone or something, every Christian needs to face the reality that God wants us to have faith in Him, and confidence is a by-product of our faith. God cares for us and wants us to have great confidence in Him. The Bible does not tell us to believe in ourselves. It teaches us to believe in Christ, to have faith and trust in God. Our confidence must be in God, and not ourselves.

Psalm 118:8 tells us, "It is better to trust in the Lord [Jehovah] than to put confidence in man." God is on your side. Psalm 118:6 says, "The Lord is on my side; I will not fear: what can man do unto me?" God is for you, not against you! The people in our lives can disappoint us, abandon us, or even turn on us. Not God! God is faithful. He has promised never to leave us or forsake us!

Christians need to wake up to the reality of a powerful God in their lives! Like David, Solomon, Peter and John, we have the ability to live confidently in this present world as we place our confidence and trust in the Lord.[2]

Millie has faced many challenges. Her circumstances reminded me of Paul's testimony while in a

Roman jail. While he was incarcerated, he wrote several letters, one being a letter to the saints in Philippi. Instead of complaining, he was rejoicing. Why? Because people would hear the good news of the Gospel. No doubt, the believers in Philippi were concerned for Paul's well-being, and his letter was intended to calm their fears and reassure them God was in control of his life.

How confident was Paul?

He was so confident in the Lord that he could assure the saints at Philippi: "Being confident of this very thing, that he which hath begun a good work in you will perform it until the day of Jesus Christ" (1:6). This verse promises that what God started in our lives will one day be completed. As the old saying goes, "God never starts something He doesn't finish!"

There are no unfinished works with God. Go all the way back to the beginning of Creation. In Genesis 2:1 we are told, "Thus the heavens and the earth were finished, and all the host of them." The work of salvation was begun in the person of Jesus Christ, and we hear Him exclaim on the cross, "It is finished!" (John 19:30). What God started in our lives will one day be completed, and the glorious work of salvation will be done. We will stand before Him and hear Him say, "It is finished!" Years ago, I heard a preacher say, "Whatever begins in grace always ends in glory!"

***

Paul's confidence led him to testify that in spite of things not working out the way he had envisioned, giving up was not an option. In spite of hardships and disappointments, he learned how to turn "his disappointments" into "His appointments!"

Look at this testimony:

Philippians 1:12-18

But I would ye should understand, brethren, that the things which happened unto me have fallen out rather unto the furtherance of the gospel; so that my bonds in Christ are manifest in all the palace, and in all other places; and many of the brethren in the Lord, waxing confident by my bonds, are much more bold to speak the word without fear. Some indeed preach Christ even of envy and strife; and some also of good will: The one preach Christ of contention, not sincerely, supposing to add affliction to my bonds: But the other of love, knowing that I am set for the defence of the gospel. What then? notwithstanding, every way, whether in pretence, or in truth, Christ is preached; and I therein do rejoice, yea, and will rejoice.

If you are looking for "gloom and doom," you won't find it in his letter. Instead, you will find a man who was seeing opportunities in his difficulties, not difficulties in his opportunities!

He gave testimony to at least three opportunities:

1. The Good News Was Exclaimed

He said, *But I would ye should understand, brethren, that the things which happened unto me have fallen out rather unto the furtherance of the gospel; so that my bonds in Christ are manifest in all the palace, and in all other places* (vv. 12-13).

51

His chains did not hinder him from preaching the Gospel.

Notice the phrase, "that the things which *happened* unto me." Most Bible scholars agree that word *happened* is not in the original text. It might have been added for clarity or context, but what it did was give the impression that things "just happen" in the lives of Christians. Paul certainly did not feel that his circumstances were the result of a capricious God who cared not for what was going on in his life. Paul viewed his imprisonment as an opportunity to exclaim the gospel of Jesus Christ to those who have never heard.

Years later, during what turned out to be the final imprisonment, he was still not complaining about his dire circumstance. He said to Timothy, "Wherein I suffer trouble, as an evil doer, even unto bonds; but the word of God is not bound" (2 Timothy 2:9). The devil thought by putting Paul in chains it would stop him from preaching the Gospel. Instead of stopping him, it opened more doors!

His chains did not hinder him from pioneering the Gospel.

Paul painted a word picture with the phrase "furtherance of the gospel" (Philippians 1:12). The word *furtherance* literally means "to cut before." The definition of the word means to "blaze a trail before the advance of an Army." The great apostle viewed himself as a "trailblazer" who was willing to go into uncharted territory.

He blazed a trail right into the heart of the seat of imperial power, the Roman government. "So that my bonds in Christ are manifest in all the palace, and in all other places" (v. 13). Paul had the vision to reach as many people as possible, and he realized that his imprisonment was an opportunity not to be ignored. He desired to reach into places that would seem impossible on the surface. Who would have ever thought that this humble preacher would one day stand before the pinnacle of power in the known world, the emperor of Rome!

The word *palace* probably refers to the praetorian guard. These 10,000-strong "best of the best" soldiers were handpicked by the emperor to be his official bodyguard. Historians tell us that more than likely Paul was guarded by Roman soldiers twenty-four hours a day. We are also told that in the normal course of events, every six hours there would be a "shift change" where every guard was replaced by another.

Can you imagine a Roman soldier, who worshiped false gods, chained to this Holy Ghost preacher? Every new guard was another opportunity to declare the good news of Jesus Christ. Soon, the word spread throughout the palace, and many were won to Christ. His statement in Philippians 4:22 gave us more reason to believe his preaching was successful: "All the saints salute you, chiefly they that are of *Caesar's household.*"

Like Paul, Millie Lumiti does not allow obstacles to stand in her way of exclaiming the Gospel. Whether it is spending all of her money to buy supplies, or traveling eight hours to get to a prison, she will not be shackled by the chains of disappointments. She is one of God's "trailblazers" who is fearless to declare, "Follow me!"

2. Christians Were Encouraged

Paul's faithfulness was an example for others to speak boldly without fear. "And many of the brethren in the

Lord, waxing confident by my bonds, are much more bold to speak the word without fear" (Philippians 1:14).

Paul's boldness inspired courage.

The word *speak* is not referring to "preaching" the Gospel in the traditional way, but rather "talking" the Gospel. It means having a conversation. Some people think that unless you stand behind a pulpit, you cannot be effective for Christ. It is a fact that more people are won to Christ by everyday conversation than any other means. Sharing a personal testimony, one-on-one, is the greatest weapon we have as Christians.

The early church did not spread the fire of the Gospel because a group of apostles decided to branch out and plant churches outside the city of Jerusalem. Actually, it wasn't the apostles who carried the good news at all.

After the death of Stephen, a flood of evil was unleashed against the early church (see Acts 8). The disciples were scattered like a seed to the regions beyond Jerusalem. The Bible says, "Therefore they that were scattered abroad went every where preaching the word" (v. 4). The apostles stayed at home while the believers carried the message of Christ to the known world. Everywhere these young Christians went, they *talked* the Gospel to anyone and everyone.

Now, fast-forward to the church at Rome. These believers were, no doubt, watching Paul witness under extreme stress and their fear was turned into boldness. It is as if these folks looked at Paul's example and said, "If he can speak the Gospel under these terrible conditions, so can we." The courage of one man stiffened their backbones!

Paul's boldness also inspired criticism.

It is hard to imagine that "some indeed preach Christ even of envy and strife; and some also of good will: The one preach Christ of contention, not sincerely, supposing to add affliction to my bonds" (Philippians 1:15-16).

Apparently, not everyone was happy that Paul was winning lost people to Jesus. Bible historians have said that the church in Rome was divided. Some wanted to help Paul win souls, while others wanted to hinder Paul and cause him more stress . . . "to add affliction to my bonds." The word *contention* is very interesting to me. It means "to run a campaign, or to promote yourself so that others will support you." In the old days, we called that, "pressing the flesh to get votes."

It would seem these so-called leaders in Rome were promoting themselves to be very important. These power-hungry "turf shepherds" would do anything to protect their little kingdoms, even to the point of stopping Paul's ministry. You know the kind? They think they are the only ones who have a "voice" and must approve what everybody else is doing for the kingdom of God. It's called "our way or the highway" type of ministry. Their jealousy and bitterness caused them to be more willing to create division within the local church than lose prominence outside the church.

What was Paul's reaction to their carping criticism, bitterness, and jealousy? He said, "What then? notwithstanding, every way, whether in pretence, or in truth, Christ is preached; and I therein do rejoice, yea, and will rejoice" (v. 18). He did not return hate for hate, or bitterness for bitterness. Instead, he said he didn't care who got the credit, or what others did or said, as long as Christ is proclaimed, and people are saved. What a wonderful attitude! We need more of that kind of grace and love in the modern church.

Millie, like Paul, was no stranger to that type of adversity. Her husband deserted the family and left them with nothing. As a single mother she lives in near poverty conditions, and yet I have never heard one negative word come out of her mouth. Millie has endured intense efforts to stop her from ministering in prisons, as well as criticism and intimidation by others who are motivated by jealousy. You name it, she has seen it!

3. Christt Was Exalted_

Paul viewed his adversity as an opportunity for Christ to be exalted. The word he used is *magnified*. His goal was to lift up and exalt the Son of God. "For I know that this shall turn to my salvation through your prayer, and the supply of the Spirit of Jesus Christ, according to my earnest expectation and my hope, that in nothing I shall be ashamed, but that with all boldness, as always, so now also Christ shall be magnified in my body, whether it be by life, or by death" (vv. 19-20).

Christ was exalted by Paul's witness.

Jesus wants to be magnified to the world. "Christ shall be magnified in my body." Christ needs a body to show Himself to a lost world. He wants to use us to do that. You may think, *How can mere mortals ever hope to magnify the Son of God?* It will happen when we surrender our bodies entirely to Him (see Romans 12:1-2).

Author Guy H. King said:

There are two kinds of magnification. One is a microscope—that makes the little seems big. With this the Christian has nothing to do, for there is nothing little about his Lord. The other way to magnify is by using a telescope. This takes that which is far away and brings it near. We are to take Jesus, so far away to this world, and bring Him near.[3]

Whether in life or death, we must be willing to do whatever it takes for others to see Christ in us. The destiny of each Christian, first and foremost, is to lift up and magnify the name of Jesus. Christ said in John 12:32, "And I, if I be lifted up from the earth, will draw all men unto me." Millie Lumiti has gone into some of the most dangerous prisons in the world. She is an example of someone who is sold out to lift up and magnify Christ.

*Christ was exalted by Paul's attitude.

Perhaps you might think it was easy for Paul to have a positive attitude—he just doesn't understand what problems I have. Really? When Paul wrote his letter, he was not in a five-star hotel in Rome. He was in a dark prison, chained like a common thief. He had no idea if his case would lead to his release from prison or would lead him to the "chopping block!" It didn't matter to him as long as people were being saved. As you read his words, you can sense his heartbeat. His attitude was one of joy, not depression; confidence, not defeat.

He used the word *joy* or *rejoicing* some eighteen times in the letter. His letter is overflowing with joy. Sadly, many believers have not learned the secret of joy. They think that *happiness* and *joy* are the same thing. Wrong.

Happiness is tied to circumstances, while *joy* is fixed on a relationship with the One who is living inside of us.

Happiness says: "My bills are paid; the kids are good; and as long as things are going my way, I am a happy camper." If your life revolves around "things going your way," you are going to spend a lot of days wallowing in the pit of discouragement.

Joy says: "No matter the circumstances, no matter if things don't go my way; I will still rejoice in the Lord of my salvation."

Consider Jesus. As He faced the cruel death of Calvary, He could say to His disciples: "These things have I spoken unto you, that my joy might remain in you, and that your joy might be full" (John 15:11). Every Christian can tap into the reservoir of joy by being in God's presence. "Thou wilt shew me the path of life: in thy presence is fulness of joy; at thy right hand there are pleasures for evermore" (Psalm 16:11).

The key to walking in joy and dealing with the hardships of life is our attitude of the heart. When we look at the example of Millie Lumiti and wonder how she could do the things that she does with such a positive attitude I am reminded of what Nehemiah told his fellow-laborers: "The joy of the Lord is your strength" (Nehemiah 8:10).

It is only through a personal relationship with Christ that we can have the confidence needed to live a life of joy and purpose. Which begs the question: How confident are you in your relationship with Christ? If you are not sure, why not bow your head, ask Jesus to forgive you of your sins, and invite Him into your heart.

It is one decision you will never regret!

DISCUSSION QUESTIONS

1. Discuss the difference between *overconfidence* and *self-confidence*. Was Paul overconfident when he said, "*I can do all things* through Christ which strengtheneth me" (Philippians 4:13)? If not, why not?

2. Why do you think ministers face jealousy and criticism (like Millie Lumiti and the Apostle Paul)?

3. What ingredients are necessary to walk in the fullness of joy? (read again Psalm 16:11; John 15:11).

4. What is the difference between being *happy* and being *joyful*? Discuss from your own personal experiences.

5. Why does Jesus Christ need us to magnify Him to the world? Couldn't He do that all by Himself? Discuss this in light of Romans 12:1-2.

NOTES

1. Definition of *confidence, Baker's Evangelical Dictionary of Biblical Theology,* online addition: *https://www.biblestudytools.com/dictionary/confidence/* (accessed October 25, 2018).

2. Pastor Ron Thomas, from a sermon titled "Christian Reality: You Can Be Confident in God!"

http://www.gospelweb.net/ronsermons4/ youcanbeconfidentingod.htm

(accessed October 25, 2018).

3. Guy H. King, *Joy Way: An Expositional Application of the Epistle to the Philippians* (Fort Washington, PA: Christian Literature Crusade, 1952) 34.

Chapter 4

SACRIFICE

Henry Taton

But to do good and to communicate forget not: for with such sacrifices God is well pleased
(Hebrews 13:16).

I believe the meaning of *sacrifice* is the willingness to put our best interests on the back burner to place God and His kingdom at the top of our priority list. Psalm 37:4 tells us, "Delight thyself also in the Lord: and he shall give thee the desires of thine heart." When we prioritize Christ, we often find that our desires change. It is the Matthew 6:33 principle of putting the kingdom of God above all else. Jesus said, "But seek ye first the kingdom of God, and his righteousness; and all these things shall be added unto you."

For many years, my dear friend, and fellow companion, Henry Taton has lived the two scriptures I've referenced above. For almost twenty years I have had the privilege of working with and observing his sacrificial life. He has led by example, and is a model of what I call "sacrificial leadership." Pastor Henry has served in several roles through the years all successfully. Henry has not been afraid of doing whatever is necessary to get the job done.

Henry Taton is an excellent example of "appearances can be deceiving." Not a very big man, he can give someone (who doesn't know him) the impression that he's not very capable of doing the things he has done. Year after year, mile after mile, construction project after construction project, he has shown all of us what sacrificial servanthood looks like; and believe me, he has never been afraid of getting his hands dirty!

Henry has traveled with me to help construct and oversee new church buildings in some of the most difficult places you can imagine. One of the most challenging areas to build a new church is a place called the Darién Gap. This area is a large swath of undeveloped swampland and forest and is within Panama's Darién Province in Central America and the northern portion of Colombia's Chocó Department in South America. It is no myth that the area is known as one of the most dangerous pieces of land in all of Central America. It is not uncommon to hear about drug smuggling, torture, or even the murder of missionaries. We thought, *"What a perfect place to build new churches!"*

The only way to get to the Darién Gap is by boat, and most of the time our mode of travel was a dugout canoe. These 45-foot-long "logs" are outfitted with twin outboard motors, and it usually takes around twelve hours to reach our destination. If you haven't sat on a plastic coke case, fought with mosquitos, and bailed water out of the bottom of the boat, then you haven't lived! Sitting there with the rest of the team is Henry Taton, and in spite of the hardships, I have never heard one word of complaint come out of his mouth.

***

The sacrifice and courage of Henry Taton is but one of our many leaders who have laid their lives on the line for the gospel of Christ.

In the Book of Philippians, the Apostle Paul mentioned a man who demonstrated the same sacrifice and courage. His name was Epaphroditus. I see many similarities between Paul's description of Epaphroditus and my friend, and co-laborer, Henry Taton.

Let's take a minute and examine why Paul pointed him out, and what made him such a valuable asset:

Philippians 2:25-30

Yet I supposed it necessary to send to you Epaphroditus, my brother, and companion in labour, and fellowsoldier, but your messenger, and he that ministered to my wants. For he longed after you all, and was full of heaviness, because that ye had heard that he had been sick. For indeed he was sick nigh unto death: but God had mercy on him; and not on him only, but on me also, lest I should have sorrow upon sorrow. I sent him therefore the more carefully, that, when ye see him again, ye may rejoice, and that I may be the less sorrowful. Receive him therefore in the Lord with all gladness; and hold such in reputation: Because for the work of Christ he was nigh unto death, not regarding his life, to supply your lack of service toward me.

Epaphroditus means "lovely," or "handsome." Not a very common name, to say the least, but the very definition of his name tells us a great deal about him. Even though we don't know very much about his background, it seems he was a trusted leader in the church at Philippi. Some have suggested that this man received the greatest honor in Paul's letter because he was willing to risk his life to bring a love gift to Paul, who was imprisoned in Rome.

Philippians 4:18 tells us, "But I have all, and abound: I am full, having received of Epaphroditus the things which were sent from you, an odour of a sweet smell, a sacrifice acceptable, wellpleasing to God."

Why was this man so honored? You don't have to look very far, or read between the lines to know the answer. It was his unselfish commitment to the cause of Christ, even to the point of death, that led Paul to elevate him as an example for the world to see. Like Epaphroditus, Henry Taton, is the kind of man every church needs to reach the world for Jesus Christ.

Let's look at three things Paul said about this man that made him a "lovely" Christian.

1. Epaphroditus Was a Balanced Man

In Philippians 2:25, we see the portrait of a well-balanced believer: "Yet I supposed it necessary to send to you Epaphroditus, *my brother*, and *companion* in *labour*, and *fellowsoldier*, but your messenger, and he that ministered to my wants." Sadly, many Christians are out of balance. It often happens when we are so engaged in one area of the faith we neglect other, just as important, aspects of living for Christ. The Lord does not intend for us to live our lives as "sprinters," but "long-distance" runners. For us to have good success, we must live a balanced life.

In Philippians 1, Paul made three statements that jump out at you. He talked about . . .

- *the fellowship of the Go*spel (v. 5)
- *the furtherance of the Gospel* (v. 12)
- *the faith of the Gospel* (v. 27).

These statements show what a well-balanced Christian looks like, and Epaphroditus fits the description of all three!

He was a "brother . . . in the fellowship of the Gospel.

Becoming a "brother in the fellowship of the gospel" is not joining some exclusive organization based on political views, or service projects in the community with organizations such as the Lions Club, and so forth. Christianity is much more than that. It is about joining together people from all walks of life who have been washed in the blood of Christ (see Ephesians 2:12-22). The common bond of Christianity is in one person, and His name is Jesus Christ.

A well-balanced Christian will desire to spend time with other believers. When I gave my life to Christ, I was born into the family of God. It is a natural thing to want to spend time with those who are like-minded. It is true that our companions tell a great deal about us. If a person professes to be saved, yet has no desire to spend time with other believers, I have to wonder whether or not they have been born again. Salvation brings us into fellowship first with Jesus Christ, and then with each other. Philippians 2:1-2 says, "If there be therefore any consolation in Christ, if any comfort of love, if any fellowship of the Spirit, if any bowels and mercies, Fulfil ye my joy, that ye be likeminded, having the same love, being of one accord, of one mind."

Pastor James Montgomery Boice writes:

Do we have such a brotherhood in the Church of Jesus Christ today? If it exists, can men and women

*see it as they saw the brotherhood of the earliest
Christians? Can they see that there is a unity among
people who profess Christ but who, from the world's
point of view, should be divided because of their
various backgrounds? I am sure such a brotherhood
exists. But I am not sure that it exists as much as it
ought to, or is as visible as it should be.*[1]

*He was a companion . . . *in the furtherance of the
Gospel.*

Paul acknowledged that Epaphroditus was blazing
the Gospel trail, standing with him shoulder to shoulder. It
should be on the agenda of every believer to share the good
news of the Gospel. Even churches can get out of balance
when they think that "fellowshipping" on Sunday is all that
is required. If we don't leave the four walls on Sunday and
take the Gospel message to where people live, we are
nothing more than a spiritual country club.

What Paul was really saying about this "brother in
the fellowship of the gospel," he was not afraid of hard
work! I am fearful that the mind-set of the church in
America is that whatever the problem may be, we can
throw some money at it, and it will take care of itself. Or, if
we talk about a problem, issue, or challenge long enough,
that is the same thing as doing something to solve whatever
the issue may be. While money is necessary, and
developing strategy is needful, it is never a wise substitute
for Christians becoming involved in changing the culture—
and that takes rolling your sleeves up and jumping in the
deep end of the pool.

Paul's commendation of Epaphroditus as a
companion in the work is reminiscent of Jesus' words to the
church at Ephesus recorded in Revelation 2. Jesus said, "I

know thy works, and thy labour, and thy patience, and how thou canst not bear them which are evil: and thou hast tried them which say they are apostles, and are not, and hast found them liars: and hast borne, and hast patience, and for my name's sake hast laboured, and hast not fainted" (vv. 2-3).

*He was a fellowsoldier . . . in fighting for the faith of the Gospel.

There is a war going on with the forces of the devil and every Christian is involved, whether we like it or not. Many people think that the Christian life is a playground, but in fact it is a battleground. We can bury our head in the sand and pretend nothing is going on, but the Word declares that when we were born again, we became a part of God's army on the earth. Paul reminded young Timothy, "Thou therefore endure hardness, as a good soldier of Jesus Christ. No man that warreth entangleth himself with the affairs of this life; that he may please him who hath chosen him to be a soldier" (2 Timothy 2:3-4; also see Ephesians 6:12). Paul was in a battle, and Epaphroditus was standing right there with him.

> A shoulder-to-shoulder fighting accounted for the success of Rome's armies. Prior to the triumph of Rome, men fought mostly as individuals. They often dressed alike and were armed alike, but they did not fight side by side with each other. The Roman armies did, and as a result the phalanxes of the legions were the terror of the ancient world. The soldiers marched abreast behind a solid wall of shields. And as they marched they struck their shields with their spears in unison and sang their battle songs. In such a way we are to advance in

harmony against the spiritual powers arrayed against us.[2]

The greatest example of living a balanced life is found in the life of Jesus Christ. Luke 2:52 tells us, "Jesus grew in wisdom and stature, and in favor with God and man" (NIV). This scripture is recorded about Jesus immediately after His return from His trip to Jerusalem, where He was noticed to be missing. His parents found Him at the Temple reasoning with the priests. We don't see Jesus again in Scripture until He is a grown man, but we have been given a glimpse of what was going on during the "silent period."

He was growing up, and maturing. He became *the* model of how a life should look when it is in proper balance. The four characteristics of Jesus' growth should become our model for balance. When these areas are in order in our lives, we will find a structure that leads to fulfillment.

1. *Jesus grew in* wisdom—*that is the* mental *side of balance.* Proverbs 23:7 declares, "For as [a man] thinketh in his heart, so is he." If you want to change the course of your life, then it will require a change in the way you think (see Romans 12:1-2).

2. *Jesus grew in* stature—*that is the* physical *side of balance.* First Corinthians 6:19-20 says, "What? know ye not that your body is the temple of the Holy Ghost which is in you, which ye have of God, and ye are not your own? For ye are bought with a price: therefore glorify God in your body, and in your spirit, which are God's." We need to understand that our bodies are truly the temple of the Holy Spirit and there is a connection between how we treat our bodies and the balance of our lives.

3. *Jesus grew in favor* with God—*that is the* spiritual *side of balance.* Second Peter 3:18 says, "But grow in grace, and in the knowledge of our Lord and Saviour Jesus Christ." Only the balance of the head and the heart will produce true spiritual growth. Spirituality is more than head knowledge; it is growing to be more like Jesus in attitude and action.

4. *Jesus grew in favor with God* and man—*that is the* social *side of balance.* Romans 12:18 says, "If it be possible, as much as lieth in you, live peaceably with all men." We must take inventory to keep our lives in balance. "The wisdom of the prudent is to give thought to their ways, but the folly of fools is deception" (Proverbs 14:8 NIV).

2. Epaphroditus Was a Burdened Man

In Philippians 2:26 we see that he had a *heaviness* of heart: "For he longed after you all, and was full of heaviness, because that ye had heard that he had been sick." The word *heaviness* means "not at home," or "to be in distress of the mind." It is the same word used when speaking about Jesus in the Garden of Gethsemane in Matthew 26:37: "And he took with him Peter and the two sons of Zebedee, and began to be sorrowful and very heavy." It would appear that Epaphroditus had his own Gethsemane experience.

Epaphroditus was burdened for several things, and it motivated him to get involved. A real burden from the Lord will always move us to action.

He was burdened *for the man of God.*

Epaphroditus refused to sit on the sidelines while his church (in Philippi) needed to send a gift to Paul. He

70

put aside his own needs and made the arduous journey to find the prison where Paul was being kept. He could have stayed at home, and let others carry the load, but he didn't. He could have said it was not a convenient time to go, but he didn't. He could have said he had already sacrificed enough, but he didn't. Epaphroditus didn't just drop a few dollars into an offering plate for some missionary in a distant land. No, he didn't just give to the offering for Paul, he gave himself to bring the offering to Paul. How did the apostle view the offering that was delivered to him? He said, "But I have all, and abound: I am full, having received of Epaphroditus the things which were sent from you, an odour of a sweet smell, a sacrifice acceptable, wellpleasing to God" (Philippians 4:18).

I am afraid we have come to a place in our churches where we take the men and women of God for granted. There are no perfect churches, and certainly, that includes those of us who stand behind the pulpit. But, that should not prevent us from praying for those who teach and preach the Word. The next time you want to go to someone and criticize your pastor, why not talk to God first and see what He has to say? You might be surprised at the answer!

He was burdened *for his church.*

This passage says Epaphroditus got sick. We don't know what his sickness was, but it was so severe it almost cost him his life. When Epaphroditus learned that his home church found out he was sick, he became burdened for them, and how they were taking the news rather than concern for himself. He believed in the local church, and so do I.

The psalmist declared in 84:10, "For a day in thy courts is better than a thousand. I had rather be a doorkeeper in the house of my God, than to dwell in the tents of wickedness." I wonder what it would be like if the spirit of Epaphroditus flooded our churches? I believe we would see a revival that would shake our cities.

He was burdened for lost souls.

The Scriptures say, "He was sick nigh unto death" (Philippians 2:27). Some Bible scholars have suggested that he got sick while witnessing to lost people in the slums of Rome. Ponder what Paul said about this giant of a soul-winner. He not only was sick unto death but *did not regard his own life* for the opportunity to win others to Christ. The literal meaning of the phrase is "gambling one's life for the Gospel." I heard someone say that Epaphroditus was one of God's gamblers who was "all in" risking his life so others might be saved!

Henry Taton, like Epaphroditus, is burdened for lost souls. After the construction of a new church building in Pinagana, Henry demonstrated something that many leaders only talk about . . . a willingness to sacrifice so others might hear the good news of Christ. He moved from Panama City, leaving his family and the comfort of a modern city, to pastor this new church located in the heart of the jungle. Why would he do that? Simple. He wanted to make sure this new congregation was established as a beacon of light sharing the gospel of Christ. He never asked for compensation or even the promise of help. He never displayed an attitude of "What's in for me?" that is so common among many of our leaders. No matter the cost, Henry was willing to pay the price. That's what sacrifice looks like!

3. Epaphroditus Was a Blessed Man

The life of Epaphroditus was a great blessing to the man of God. He stood in the place of an entire church and brought a love offering to Paul at the risk of his own life. Paul told the church when they see him again they will rejoice and be glad. "Therefore I am all the more eager to send him, so that when you see him again you may be glad and I may have less anxiety" (Philippians 2:28 NIV). What a wonderful thing to say about the godly influence of someone; every Christian should desire to be a blessing to others.

David Livingstone gave his life to open up Africa to the gospel of Christ, and according to history he became the first European to traverse the width of Africa.

John Piper, founder of *Desiring God*, observed:

Many doubted Livingstone's sincerity as a missionary since he spent so much of his time exploring. But his own perspective was clear: "As for me, I am determined to open up Africa or perish." He said, "The end of the exploration is the beginning of the enterprise." A year before he died in 1873, he wrote in his journal on his 59th birthday, "My birthday! My Jesus, my King, my Life, my All. I again dedicate my whole self to Thee."[3]

On December 4, 1857, David Livingstone addressed the students of Cambridge University about "leaving the benefits of England behind."

He said:

For my own part, I have never ceased to rejoice that God has appointed me to such an office. People talk of the sacrifice I have made in spending so much of

*my life in Africa. Can that be called a sacrifice
which is simply paid back as a small part of a great
debt owing to our God, which we can never repay?
Is that a sacrifice which brings its own blest reward
in healthful activity, the consciousness of doing
good, peace of mind, and a bright hope of a
glorious destiny hereafter? Away with the word in
such a view, and with such a thought! It is
emphatically no sacrifice. Say rather it is a
privilege. Anxiety, sickness, suffering, or danger,
now and then, with a foregoing of the common
conveniences and charities of this life, may make us
pause, and cause the spirit to waver, and the soul to
sink; but let this only be for a moment. All these are
nothing when compared with the glory which shall
be revealed in and for us. I never made a sacrifice.*[4]

Only eternity will reveal the influence of a godly life. Someone once commented, "Our lives are like a rock thrown in a lake, the ripples continue to reach out." Men like Epaphroditus, Henry Taton, and so many more, continue to demonstrate what sacrificial leadership looks like. I pray God will give us more who are infused with the same spirit—AMEN!

DISCUSSION QUESTIONS

1. There were many others who helped Paul during his ministry. Why do you think he chose to highlight Epaphroditus as an example of sacrifice?

2. Briefly describe what the term *sacrificial leadership* means to you.

3. If you had the opportunity to travel with Henry Taton in a canoe for twelve hours to share the Gospel, would you? Explain your answer—yes or no.

4. Can you point to any examples of Christians getting "out of balance"?

5. How would you explain to a new Christian the term *fellow-soldier* in Christ?

NOTES

1. James Montgomery Boice, *An Expositional Commentary —Philippians* (Grand Rapids, MI: Zondervan Publishing, 1971) 181.

2. Boice, 184.

3. John Piper, *I Never Made a Sacrifice, https:// www.desiringgod.org/articles/i-never-made-a-sacrifice* (accessed December 1, 2018).

4. David Livingstone, Speech to students at Cambridge University (4 December 1857), *https://en.wikiquote.org/ wiki/David_Livingstone* (accessed December 1, 2018).

Chapter 5
COURAGE
Brother Moses

Be strong and of a good courage, fear not, nor be afraid of them: for the Lord thy God, he it is that doth go with thee; he will not fail thee, nor forsake thee (Deuteronomy 31:6).

I will call him Brother Moses. That's not his real name. It is my way of protecting him from those who would try to stamp out his witness for Christ. Brother Moses lives and ministers in a country that is almost 99% Buddhist, and where religious persecution is common; therefore, to reveal his name and location might put him in danger. Churches in his country are under the strict control of a communist government, and it requires real courage to preach Christ. When the government tried to force his ministry to register, Brother Moses refused. In years past he did prison time because of the Gospel, but that did not stop him from preaching.

The history of his country is one of violence, poverty, and war. As a young boy, he lived with his family beside an Air Force base that was bombed by the communist government. All of his family members were killed in the bombing, and he was severely wounded, but by God's grace, he survived. Soon after that missionaries came and ministered to him, not only physically, but also spiritually; eventually, they led this young man to Christ. Brother Moses has felt the pain of loss as few have felt, but it has not stopped him from taking a courageous stand for Christ.

Against all the odds, this lion of God has not allowed fear to paralyze or stop him from following the vision God gave him. Courage comes in many shapes and sizes, and the attribute of courage has many descriptions and definitions. But, for me when I think of raw courage, I can think of no better example than my friend Brother Moses. He does not back away from taking responsibility, whether it is overseeing underground churches or leading an orphanage. His courageous sacrifice is evident even when he knows the authorities are watching him, or faced with the threat of another imprisonment.

The first time I met anyone from his ministry was when we held a conference, not in his country, but across the border in a neighboring country more open to Christianity. Brother Moses was scheduled to attend, and I was looking forward to meeting him. But, he was denied permission to leave. Only his wife and some of his team were able to attend.

I have found that courage is contagious. Some of the places we go requires a great deal of courage, and quite frankly, some people won't go if there is an element of danger involved. Whenever you have the privilege of serving with someone who is as courageous as Brother Moses, their courage will inevitably rub off on you. His attitude is best described by Paul in Romans 8:31: "What shall we then say to these things? If God be for us, who can be against us?"

In his book *Becoming a Leader*, Myles Munroe said that J. Oswald Sanders defines *courage* as "the quality of mind which enables men to encounter danger and difficulty with firmness, and without fear or depression."[1]

Munroe also reflected on his life as a leader:

For years and years I used to pray for strength and guess what, I never got an ounce. Why? Because all the strength you need, you already have. Courage is standing up on your strength. Courage is resistance to and mastery of fear, not the absence of fear. All leaders encounter the complexity of fear, but they are never immobilized by it, they use it to motivate their potential. This is courage.[2]

Brother Moses, though small in stature, stands tall in this regard. Yes, leadership requires a measure of courage, as Billy Graham once famously said: "When a brave man takes a stand, the spines of others are often stiffened!" The Bible, as well as the pages of human history, are filled with men and women who, when faced with fearful circumstances, prevailed.

I love the adage that says, "A ship in the harbor is safe, but that is not what ships are built for." Safety, security, and survival are not meaningful goals for our lives. If we are going to get anywhere, there comes the point when we have to trust God for the unknown. I find that Brother Moses lives his life as that ship sailing in the open waters unafraid of what storms may come.

***

There is a story in Scripture about a young champion who displayed similar courage to that of Brother Moses. His name was David. This sheepherder turned warrior stood in the presence of professional soldiers—who were trembling in fear at the sight of a giant named Goliath

—and said: "Is there not a cause?" (1 Samuel 17:29). David was asking a simple question, but it was pregnant with eternal consequences: "Is there not a reason to fight?"

My friend Brother Moses is that kind of warrior. When giants show up, he meets them with faith and is not paralyzed by fear or unbelief.

David's amazing story is found in 1 Samuel 17. Let's take a trip to the Valley of Elah. On one side of the valley is the army of King Saul. Arrayed in battle formation on the other side of the valley is the army of the Philistines. There is a fight brewing, and unless the Lord intervenes, this is going to be a slaughter.

I see at least FIVE lessons in leadership courage.

Lesson #1—*Be Faithful* (To your assignment)

1 Samuel 16:13-14

Then Samuel took the horn of oil, and anointed him in the midst of his brethren: and the Spirit of the Lord came upon David from that day forward. So Samuel rose up, and went to Ramah. But the Spirit of the Lord departed from Saul, and an evil spirit from the Lord troubled him.

Viewing the fight between David and Goliath in context is important. David was not some random teenager who just decided to go down and watch the action. By the time he appeared on the scene, he had been anointed king.

His destiny was to be king, but his immediate assignment was to obey his father. Instead of trying to start a new ministry or announcing to the world that he is the new king of Israel, he is simply tending sheep. I can find no evidence David was doing anything other than what his father, Jesse, had assigned him to do. He is faithful to bloom where he's planted. He is fully content to a be a faithful son, a willing servant, playing his harp and looking after the sheep. I have a feeling being anointed king was as much as a surprise to him as to any of his family. One of David's greatest *abilities* was his *dependability.* He could be counted on to stand his post, and not waver.

No doubt in my mind, that is why God chose him. He was faithful in the "natural" things so at some point God could trust him in the greater spiritual things. One of these days God's people are going to wake up and realize that before God will use us in the big things, we must learn to be faithful in the small things (see Luke 16:10-13). Where did we ever get the idea that when God's call is on our life, we no longer have to be concerned with such trivial matters as cutting the grass or helping out in the kitchen? To some "superspiritual" saints paying bills on time, or helping out on a workday at the church, doesn't seem nearly as important as hearing that one day they will travel the world preaching the Gospel.

Remember, when David was anointed king, Saul still had the title. God's rejection of Saul was mostly unknown to the rest of the people. He was good at putting up a front, but sooner rather than later, God's judgment was going to be known by everyone. The favor and blessing of God were removed from Saul. *He had the title, but David had the anointing.*

At some point, we, like David, will face our own giant. It may be a marital issue, a health problem, or a financial meltdown; whatever name you want to give it, everyone is going to face a giant sooner or later. They may not all be over nine feet tall, but trust me, when you're facing one it may appear to be. A *giant* is: *any circumstance, person, or thing that stands in your way of completing your assignment.* These obstacles must be confronted by the power of God.

Lesson #2—*Be Fearless* (Replace fear with faith)

1 Samuel 17:8-11

And he stood and cried unto the armies of Israel, and said unto them, Why are ye come out to set your battle in array? Am not I a Philistine, and ye servants to Saul? Choose you a man for you, and let him come down to me. If he be able to fight with me, and to kill me, then will we be your servants: but if I prevail against him, and kill him, then shall ye be our servants, and serve us. And the Philistine said, I defy the armies of Israel this day; give me a man, that we may fight together. When Saul and all Israel heard those words of the Philistine, they were dismayed, and greatly afraid.

Imagine the scene. Fifteen miles west of Bethlehem the armies of Israel and the armies of the Philistines were gathered together for battle. Every morning the Philistines trotted out their champion Goliath to challenge Saul's army. Just the mention of the name Goliath brought paralyzing fear. No ordinary warrior, he would have been about nine feet, nine inches tall; his armor consisted of a bronze helmet, a coat of scale armor weighing about 125 pounds, and a pair of bronze leggings. His weapons were a bronze spear with a fifteen-pound tip, a sword, and a javelin. His shield was carried by an armor-bearer who walked before him. He was the perfect killing machine!

In those days, they had an unusual rule of combat. To prevent unnecessary loss of life, they would send out their most abled warriors to fight each other. This duel would be a representative war with the nation of the loser becoming subject to the winner. The outcome was thought to be the judgment of the gods on the matter. Thus, the fight was really between the gods of the Philistines and the God of Israel. Day after day, Goliath would challenge the army to send out a man to fight. "And the Philistine said, I defy the armies of Israel this day; give me a man, that we may fight together" (v. 10).

Meanwhile, back in the trenches, Saul's army was in a panic. Had Saul been the anointed and godly leader he should have been, he would have claimed Deuteronomy 20 and led his troops to victory.

When thou goest out to battle against thine enemies, and seest horses, and chariots, and a people more than thou, be not afraid of them: for the Lord thy God is with thee, which brought thee up out of the land of Egypt. And it shall be, when ye are come nigh unto the battle, that the priest shall approach and speak unto the people, And shall say unto them, Hear, O Israel, ye approach this day unto battle against your enemies: let not your hearts faint, fear not, and do not tremble, neither be ye terrified because of them; for the Lord your God is he that goeth with you, to fight for you against your enemies, to save you (vv. 1-4).

However, when a man is out of fellowship with God, he can't lead them anywhere but to defeat! So, you have a king in rebellion, an army that wouldn't fight, and one young man who was sent by his father to bring some food to his brothers.

You and I have a choice when a giant shows up. You can hide in fear (like Saul's army) or *you can replace fear with faith as David did.*

Faith and fear are mutually exclusive. They cannot occupy the same heart. You will either operate in faith, or you will operate in fear. When faced with our Goliath, one of the first emotions to rise to the surface is fear. Fear can be a paralyzing emotion and must be dealt with. I'm sure David, like most of us, felt a measure of fear rise up in his heart when he considered what he was about to do. Please understand that fear can be more than an emotion, it can also be a spirit that attacks us. Second Timothy 1:7 says, "For God has not given us a spirit of fear, but of power and of love and of a sound mind" (NKJV). It does not matter how much stress I endure, I am not going to live in fear of what man may do to me. I am going to walk in faith. Faith will always crowd out fear every single time.

Lesson #3—*Be Focused* (Don't listen to the critics)

1 Samuel 17:14-18

> *And David was the youngest: and the three eldest followed Saul. But David went and returned from Saul to feed his father's sheep at Bethlehem. And the Philistine drew near morning and evening, and presented himself forty days. And Jesse said unto David his son, Take now for thy brethren an ephah of this parched corn, and these ten loaves, and run to the camp of thy brethren; and carry these ten cheeses unto the captain of their thousand, and look how thy brethren fare, and take their pledge.*

Get the picture. David shows up with some lunch for his three older brothers who were soldiers in the army.

85

Jesse sent David back and forth with food continually, so it was not unusual for David to be there. David was basically an errand boy.

For forty days Goliath came out and defied the army. "And the Philistine drew near morning and evening, and presented himself forty days" (v. 16). Every time these big, tough, hardened soldiers heard Goliath's challenge, they would run and hide like frightened rabbits! King Saul did everything he could to encourage his frightened soldiers to fight. He sent out a "text" alert which read: "Any soldier who will take on Goliath and kill him will receive unlimited wealth, my beautiful daughter in marriage, and tax exemption for himself and his entire family." He put them on the "incentive" plan, but even that didn't work.

But, today it was going to be different. When David heard the challenge of Goliath, something was stirred in his spirit. David uttered his first recorded words: "What shall be done to the man that killeth this Philistine, and taketh away the reproach from Israel? For who is this uncircumcised Philistine, that he should defy the armies of the living God?" (v. 26). While the combat-hardened troops are digging their foxholes deeper, this kid is ready to get in the ring.

I wish to God we had that same attitude today. It is not us that need to be fearful about how we're going to stop the devil; it is the devil that needs to be fearful about us. If we ever figure out who we are in Jesus Christ, there is no way the forces of darkness can stop the army of the living God! You are a child of the King, and you have royal blood flowing through your veins. You don't have to run and hide from the devil anymore! It does not mean the enemy will not attack; it just means when he does, we have weapons at our disposal (see 2 Corinthians 10:3-6).

Enter Eliab. As soon as David was ready to face the "Giant problem," the devil immediately attacked him from an unexpected source. "And Eliab his eldest brother heard when he spake unto the men; and Eliab's anger was kindled against David, and he said, Why camest thou down hither? and with whom hast thou left those few sheep in the wilderness? I know thy pride, and the naughtiness of thine heart; for thou art come down that thou mightest see the battle" (1 Samuel 17:28).

David's older brother, Eliab, tried to discourage him. I thought the oldest brother always took care of the younger brother. Could it be that Eliab had his own issues? You will remember that it was *this* brother, not David, everyone expected would be anointed king. It must have been a blow to his ego to hear Samuel say, "You are not the man" (see 16:6-7).

Listening to his words of criticism to David, there is no doubt in my mind that Eliab had a jealous heart toward David. There is a national crisis brewing. The future of the nation hangs in the balance, and all he wants to do is criticize his young brother for coming to check on his family. As Woodrow Wilson said, "It is just as hard to do your duty when men are sneering at you as when they are shooting at you." And, every preacher I know can say, AMEN! Through it all, we must be like David and remain focused.

It may be a shock to your system to realize that we all have our own "Eliabs." There will always be those who are going to criticize us, especially when they think we have made a mistake. Then, when we try to do the right thing, they stand over our shoulder and criticize even that. The truth is they never seem to get in the game themselves, and they don't want us to be successful. David was focused on his assignment. He knew that something had to be done. He makes the statement, "Is there not a cause?" Even in his youth, like a laser beam, he focuses on the problem and determines to do something about it.

Two of the most effective weapons Satan will use is *fear* and *discouragement*. When fear doesn't work, he will try to topple your faith with discouragement. It usually comes through people, and in my personal experience it may come from someone closest to you. Believe it or not, Satan's favorite weapon against church people is other church people. Some people are like "water boys" on a football team. They wait until you look like you're "getting hot" and then they want to throw water in your face. There will always be those who were waiting on your success just so they can be around to cool you off when you're getting too far ahead.

The best way to avoid criticism is . . . do nothing, say nothing, and be nothing. Then someone will come along and criticize you for wasting your talent! The greatest men and women of the Bible and human history were criticized, so you're in good company.

It is obvious to me that Eliab was so jealous of David's courage that he fell into the trap of criticizing what he didn't understand. At the heart of his criticism were three accusations (1 Samuel 17:28 NIV):

1. *He accused David of pride.* "I know how conceited you are and how wicked your heart is." Eliab developed x-ray vision and looked into David's heart. It's not unusual for a critic to impugn your motives.

2. *He accused David of neglect.* "And with whom did you leave those few sheep in the desert?" Eliab was basically saying, "You should be a good little boy and go back and take care of the sheep; you have no business here."

3. *He accused David of a wicked curiosity.* "You came down only to watch the battle." No matter what David said, it was going to be wrong. So, David spoke what was in his heart, "Is there not a cause?" (v. 29). David's heart was stirred, and bold courage began to bubble up out of his spirit. He knew that shrinking back and hiding from the enemy would only lead to humiliation, destruction, defeat, and enslavement.

Lesson #4—*Be Thankful* (Celebrate past victories)

1 Samuel 17:31-37

And when the words were heard which David spake, they rehearsed them before Saul: and he sent for him. And David said to Saul, Let no man's heart fail because of him; thy servant will go and fight with this Philistine. And Saul said to David, Thou art not able to go against this Philistine to fight with him: for thou art but a youth, and he a man of war from his youth. And David said unto Saul, Thy servant kept his father's sheep, and there came a lion, and a bear, and took a lamb out of the flock: And I went out after him, and smote him, and delivered it out of his mouth: and when he arose against me, I caught him by his beard, and smote him, and slew him. Thy servant slew both the lion and the bear: and this uncircumcised Philistine shall be as one of them, seeing he hath defied the armies of the living God. David said moreover, The Lord that delivered

*me out of the paw of the lion, and out of the paw of
the bear, he will deliver me out of the hand of this
Philistine. And Saul said unto David, Go, and the
Lord be with thee.*

The lesson we need to learn is when faced with
present-day giants, remember past victories. *Too often we
remember what we should forget, and forget what we
should remember.* You see, when you remember a past
victory it will cause you to have faith for future victories.
How you handle "midget" problems will determine how
you handle the "giant" ones. If you have a meltdown when
you get a flat tire, or when the sewer backs up, what will
you do when a "giant" knocks on your door at 2 o'clock in
the morning? The reason a lot of Christians have such weak
faith is they have such short memories.

When David began to consider taking on Goliath,
he went to King Saul and told him what was in his heart. Of
course, Saul's first reaction was negative. I don't blame the
king; there was nothing in David that would suggest he had
the strength, or ability, to bring down this giant. I'm sure
the army was filled with men who had tasted battle before.
If the strongest were filled with fear, what makes this
young teenage boy think that he can tackle this problem all
by himself?

In 1 Samuel 17:32, 34-36, David answers the
challenge by citing experiences with God against a lion and
a bear. Verse 37 sums it up as far as David is concerned:
"I've seen the faithfulness of God. The same God who
delivered me from them is upon me to deliver me
now" (paraphrased).

It becomes a source of strength to know that God
did come through for us in the past. We don't celebrate

enough of the past victories that God has given us. When a new Goliath shows up in your life, what is the first thing that fills your heart? Is it fear, or faith? Is it intimidation, or celebration? If we are not careful, we will become fearful and timid just like Saul's army, afraid to take on Goliath.

Lesson #5—*Be Real* (Walk in your own anointing)

1 Samuel 17:38-40

And Saul armed David with his armour, and he put an helmet of brass upon his head; also he armed him with a coat of mail. And David girded his sword upon his armour, and he assayed to go; for he had not proved it. And David said unto Saul, I cannot go with these; for I have not proved them. And David put them off him. And he took his staff in his hand, and chose him five smooth stones out of the brook, and put them in a shepherd's bag which he had, even in a scrip; and his sling was in his hand: and he drew near to the Philistine.

David tried on the armor, and as you might suspect, it didn't fit. Saul is a size 50 and David is a size 32. But, Saul is the expert here. As David listens to him, he discovers that he can hardly move. Can't you see David dragging that big ole sword around? To meet Goliath wearing Saul's armor will be a disaster. David needs to fight the battle using what he knows. He said, in essence, "I've tested that ole sling. I know what that rock will do. And, I am confident in my throwing ability. I know this stuff works, I've already proven it." If he got close enough to Goliath to need armor, it's game over!

The lesson for us is obvious. You can't walk in someone else's anointing. David was walking in something greater than physical armor, and so are we! You may be in the fight of your life today, but remember, when it comes to the anointing, one size does not fit all. Many times, we exhaust all of our resources to find answers to deal with our giants. We go to family, friends, books, and anything else we can get our hands on to find solutions. There is nothing wrong with getting wise counsel, but when it comes to facing Goliath, we need more than counsel—we need a powerful anointing. When the pressure of circumstances is great on the outside, the Holy Spirit will give equal pressure on the inside so that there will be no cracks or "crack-ups." We can trust the Holy Spirit that whatever happens, He is there to provide everything we need.

You know how this story ends. It has been preached and written about for centuries. David scored a first-round knockout. You know it wasn't even close (1 Samuel 17:45-50).

When David looked at Goliath, he did not see a big problem covering up the face of God. On the contrary, David viewed Goliath through the lens of heaven's perspective and saw that God was bigger than his problem. Until a Goliath shows up in your life, you will end up being a shepherd boy singing to sheep until the day you die. But, you let a problem show up, and God will promote you to where He wants you to be. If you are facing a Goliath, be happy because God has allowed you to go through it.

Remember: The biggest giants produce the greatest results and rewards. As we move toward our assignment, there will be giants blocking the road ahead. Each new level will produce an even bigger enemy. It's evident that David was "training for reigning" and the next step was to take on Goliath. The sooner we learn that we have an enemy blocking our way, the better off we will be. Whatever is sent to destroy you will actually become a footstool to promote you! Don't run away from Goliath; run toward him, armed with the anointing and power of God!

I pray that God will give us more men like David, Brother Moses, and countless others who are not afraid to stand in the gap. Even when the devil sends his "Goliaths" to put out our flame of testimony, may we have the courage and boldness to say, "I won't back up, shut up, or sit down!"

DISCUSSION QUESTIONS

1. Besides the five leadership lessons listed, can you name other lessons you learned from David's defeat of Goliath?

2. Were you surprised to learn some countries persecute those who preach the Gospel? If so, why?

3. Read 1 Samuel 17:45-47. Discuss the three aspects of his victory over Goliath.

    (a) The source of his victory was _____.

    (b) The strength of his victory was _____.

    (c) The secret of his victory was _____.

4. David only needed one stone to kill Goliath—why did David take five smooth stones in his bag? Did he think he would miss? What's your explanation?

5. David didn't speak "about the giant" but directly to him. Why? Can you find other examples in Scripture of the power of the spoken word?

NOTES

1. Myles Munroe, *Becoming a Leader* (Rockville, MD: Pneuma Life Publishing, 1993) 141.

2. Munroe, 141.

Chapter 6

STEADFASTNESS

Premadasa

Therefore, my beloved brethren, be ye stedfast, unmoveable, always abounding in the work of the Lord, forasmuch as ye know that your labour is not in vain in the Lord (1 Corinthians 15:58).

I remind you that the leadership traits we are examining in this book are being unpacked in the context of ministry applications and examples in the lives of ordinary people who are doing extraordinary things. These unsung heroes have looked death in the eye as they put one foot in front of the other steadfastly following Jesus. The same principles lived out in secular circles will bring positive results; but when the motivation is to please our Savior and further the kingdom of God, we see an exponential increase of credibility and influence.

One of the most crucial traits of any successful leader is *steadfastness*. As Paul exhorted the believers in Corinth, he used two words that speak to this truth, *steadfast* and *unmovable*. According to the *Oxford English Dictionary*, the word *steadfast* is used to "connote fixed or secure in position, solid and firm in substance, unshaken, and resolute." Also, the word *unmovable* is used to indicate that a person or thing is "not subject to change, unalterable, and firmly fixed; it also suggests the quality of being unyielding and incapable of being diverted from one's purpose." Combining the two words Paul used, you see a picture of a steadfast believer as a person who is *solid, firm, resolute, firmly fixed, and incapable of being diverted from a primary purpose or mission.* It is a dogged determination that won't let you quit no matter the cost.

One of the best examples of determination and steadfastness is my friend and fellow laborer Premadasa. I choose not to divulge his full name or the country where he is serving. I do not want to give the enemy any opening to bring further persecution to him, his family, or his ministry. Premadasa serves in a predominately Buddhist country. His city is known as a Buddhist revival center. Serving Christ under the best of circumstances is a challenge, but when you face the prospect of persecution and death, it requires a certain steadfastness that few men possess. For many years, Premadasa and his entire family have faced the possibility of daily persecution, and yet few have maintained the steadfastness that I have observed in him.

As a young man, Premadasa was himself a monk headed for the highest echelon of the Buddhist faith. As a monk, you have a certain level of privilege that most people don't enjoy. But, one day he had an encounter with Jesus Christ and his life changed forever. He was willing to give up his life of worshiping before a golden statue and serve the living Christ!

In Acts 20 the Apostle Paul was making his journey back to Jerusalem. He stopped in Miletus and called for the elders of the church in Ephesus. As he spoke parting words to them, he summed up his ministry and how he viewed what was about to happen to him in Jerusalem. He said, "But none of these things move me, neither count I my life dear unto myself, so that I might finish my course with joy, and the ministry, which I have received of the Lord Jesus, to testify the gospel of the grace of God" (v. 24). As I read what Paul said about the impending danger that awaited him in Jerusalem, I cannot help but think of my friend Premadasa, who is the epitome of that scripture!

***

When I consider the steadfast life of Premadasa, I began to ask the Holy Spirit to show me a Biblical example of steadfastness that might compare. Out of many men and women in Scripture who would qualify, the life experience of Daniel was the one that kept coming to my mind.

Daniel is indeed one of those Old Testament figures that stand out. I am afraid we are so quick to jump to the lion's den that we skip over the early experiences of his life that led up to his amazing deliverance. He didn't become solid, firm, resolute, firmly fixed, and incapable of being diverted from his primary purpose or mission overnight. No, his early, steadfast decisions led to great rewards. It still works that way today.

But, first a little background.

Daniel was a young man when he was taken captive. I cannot imagine how he and the other young men felt as they were taken to the great city of Babylon. Historians tell us that the city itself was grand in every imaginable way. Even today the "Hanging Gardens" of Babylon are still known as one of the Seven Wonders of the World.

Although no one knows for a certainty, most Bible scholars agree that Daniel was probably between eighteen and twenty-five years of age when he was brought to the center of architecture, wealth, and knowledge of his day. King Nebuchadnezzar had a plan for these young men. He intended to take these young Hebrew captives, give them the best food, and the best education to build the wisest and strongest young men possible to lead his nation.

And the king spake unto Ashpenaz the master of his eunuchs, that he should bring certain of the children of Israel, and of the king's seed, and of the princes; Children in whom was no blemish, but well favoured, and skilful in all wisdom, and cunning in knowledge, and understanding science, and such as had ability in them to stand in the king's palace, and whom they might teach the learning and the tongue of the Chaldeans. And the king appointed them a daily provision of the king's meat, and of the wine which he drank: so nourishing them three years, that at the end thereof they might stand before the king (Daniel 1:3-5).

Yes, the king had a plan—but, Daniel had a different plan! Daniel's decisions became the *building blocks* on which to construct a steadfast life. Time and space won't allow for many details, but let's look at a few.

Building Block #1—He was a man of *purpose*

Now among these were of the children of Judah, Daniel, Hananiah, Mishael, and Azariah: Unto whom the prince of the eunuchs gave names: for he gave unto Daniel the name of Belteshazzar; and to Hananiah, of Shadrach; and to Mishael, of Meshach; and to Azariah, of Abednego. But Daniel purposed in his heart *that he would not defile himself with the portion of the king's meat, nor with the wine which he drank: therefore, he requested of the prince of the eunuchs that he might not defile himself. Now God had brought Daniel into favour and tender love with the prince of the eunuchs. And the prince of the eunuchs said unto Daniel, I fear my lord the king, who hath appointed your meat and*

your drink: for why should he see your faces worse
liking than the children which are of your sort? then
shall ye make me endanger my head to the king.
Then said Daniel to Melzar, whom the prince of the
eunuchs had set over Daniel, Hananiah, Mishael,
and Azariah, Prove thy servants, I beseech thee, ten
days; and let them give us pulse to eat, and water to
drink (Daniel 1:6-12).

- *It was a hard decision.*

When the king's plan was introduced to Daniel, he had to make a hard decision. I don't care how long you have been a Christian when a decision (whatever it may be) is made to stand out against the "everybody is doing it crowd," there will always be those who stand ready to condemn you.

Daniel could have said, "I am far away from home; no one will ever know if I participate or not." He would not have been the first one to say, "I want to fit in, so what's the harm?" He purposed in his heart not to defile himself with their lifestyle. To eat the king's food might not have looked very serious to others, but to Daniel, it flew in the face of his core values. He chose not to rationalize his actions, but to steadfastly reject the new meal plan.

You don't have to be a Christian very long before you realize just how subtle and deceptive the devil can be. If we avail ourselves to the proper spiritual nourishment (God's meal plan), I can guarantee you the enemy will try to insert his "meal plan" into our lives. The devil's plan only has one course—lies, wrapped in deception! When Jesus was confronted by the devil's lies, He responded: "It is written, Man shall not live by bread alone, but by every word that proceedeth out of the mouth of God" (Matthew 4:4).

Pastor James MacDonald writes:

Imagine driving to the grocery store and buying all of the ingredients for your favorite meal. Imagine measuring and mixing and cooking those ingredients until the meal is finished. Imagine dishing the meal onto your best china plates and setting them on your dining-room table—and then just leaving the food to sit. Imagine watching your favorite meal grow cold and congeal until it's no longer appetizing in any way.

That would be a tragedy, right? That would be a total waste of a good meal. And the same is true when followers of Jesus fail to dine on His Word.

It's not enough to pick up the Bible. No, you have to consume God's Word. You have to ingest it into yourself. You have to hide God's Word in your heart so that you won't sin against Him (see Psalm 119:11). That's why Jeremiah 15:16 is my life verse: "Your words were found, and I ate them, and your words became to me a joy and the delight of my heart, for I am called by your name, O Lord, God of hosts." [1]

Early on, you can see how Daniel developed a steadfast spirit. He was willing to make the right decision, based on his convictions, even when no one was looking! He must have known that to go against the order of the king would bring dire consequences. Daniel was willing to stand for what he knew was right in the face of the most powerful man on the planet. That's a hard thing to do!

We are living in a time when the church is looking more like the world, than the other way around. We should never be afraid to be different, as 1 Peter 2:9 tells us: "[We] are a chosen generation, a royal priesthood, an holy nation, a peculiar people; that [we] should shew forth the praises of [God]." Nor should we bow down at the altar of a politically correct society that seeks to deter the church from its original mandate—to preach the gospel of Christ to every creature, and make disciples of all nations (Mark 16:15; Matthew 28:18-20).

You say going against the norms is hard—sure it is —nothing worth anything is ever going to be easy. Premadasa, like Daniel in his day, is willing to make hard decisions. He, and others like him, make those decisions knowing full well that their courage and steadfastness in the face of evil could lead to death.

- *It was a heart decision.*

You could say that Daniel had "heart." If you have ever been in the presence of someone who dared to overcome obstacles and not follow the crowd, you might say they have a "truckload of guts." It merely means they are not easily swayed. Their drive, desire, and motivation keep them from peer pressure causing them to do things that are contrary to what they believe. Being different and not afraid to fight for what's right is a part of their character.

Daniel was surrounded by compromise and mediocrity but decided to discipline himself and not get caught up in the atmosphere of the city. Truth is never at the mercy of the consensus of what's right. Majority rule is not always right. Usually, those who don't have dreams or purpose in their heart are the ones who want to take a vote.

It's easy to make a group decision, and hiding in a crowd is a common characteristic of those who "go with the flow." The last time I checked, God doesn't need my approval to make decisions. When you read the Bible, you discover that He doesn't govern by the majority, because He alone is the majority. His vote is the only one that counts!

Daniel practiced something that many modern-day believers have trouble understanding—it's called *self-discipline*. It's a fact if we cannot discipline ourselves, we will never develop a steadfast spirit. Self-discipline should affect every area of our life, including the physical, spiritual, mental, and financial.

I am sure you know that *discipline* and *disciple* come from the same root word. Excitement and passion will get you out of the starting blocks, but self-discipline will keep you running in the race. It's not the ones with the most talent or the most skills that end up crossing the finish line first. It's the ones who have learned the secret of a self-disciplined lifestyle. You may have all the talent in the world, but without self-discipline, you won't last. I have said it before, and I will continue to remind you that the Christian life is a marathon, not a sprint! Falling by the wayside is a common trait of those who do not practice self-discipline.

A common denominator of self-discipline is learning to listen more than talking. It could be why God gave us two ears and one mouth—so we can listen twice as much as we talk! James 1:19 says, "Wherefore, my beloved brethren, let every man be swift to hear, slow to speak, slow to wrath."

Self-discipline and personal growth go hand-in-hand. Just like our attitude is a choice, so is self-discipline.

If you want to get something out of life, you have to put something into it. Daniel demonstrated self-discipline in more than just one or two areas of his life. Those who are disciplined in small things tend to be disciplined in large things as well, whereas those who are undisciplined will tend to be that way in almost every area of their lives.

Some may think that self-discipline is too time-consuming, rigorous, and not worth the effort. The truth is, self-discipline produces more quality time for the critical issues of your life. Besides, what better way for a leader to model the life of Christ than through self-discipline?

Daniel, along with Shadrach, Meshach, and Abednego were selected for specialized training. Their decision to refrain from the king's delicacies was already determined. Self-discipline is made easier when the decision is made beforehand and not under pressure. They knew what they would not do, so when the pressure was applied, they did not crack under strain.

- *It was a humble decision.*

These young men were under the care of the chief of the eunuchs. The king had given him free rein to train and be responsible for their assimilation into the ways of the kingdom. Daniel refused to show a rebellious attitude and did not allow bitterness and hatred to come between them. No doubt, had he taken the rebellious approach, he would have opened himself up for a different outcome.

Quite the contrary, Daniel took the approach of loving this man and building a relationship with him. Because of this, God was able to work through Daniel and create a bond between Daniel and his captor. An excellent and steadfast spirit refuses a judgmental attitude and a display of righteous indignation, while seeking to build relationships with love, even with its enemies.

Daniel's humility gave strength to his words. The late A.W. Tozer said in his book *The Pursuit of God:*

> *The humble man is not a human mouse, suffering a sense of his own inferiority. In his moral life, he may be as bold as a lion and as strong as Samson, but he doesn't fool himself about himself. He has accepted God's estimate with regard to his own life. He knows he is as weak and as helpless as God has declared him to be. Paradoxically, he relies on the confidence that in the sight of God, he is more important than the angels. In himself, he is nothing; in God, he is everything. That's his motivating motto.* [2]

Building Block #2—He was a man of *prayer*

The Bible leaves no doubt about one thing—Daniel was a praying man: "Now when Daniel knew that the writing was signed, he went into his house; and his windows being open in his chamber toward Jerusalem, he kneeled upon his knees three times a day, and prayed, and gave thanks before his God, *as he did aforetime*" (Daniel 6:10).

- *He started his day in prayer.*

We are told Daniel prayed three times a day in his special prayer chamber atop his house. He had a set time and a special place to meet with God. The psalmist declared, "Evening, and morning, and at noon, will I pray, and cry aloud: and he shall hear my voice" (Psalm 55:17). It was a good thing that Daniel started his day in prayer, because little did he know that the devil was already laying plans to present him with the most challenging test of his life, and his strong prayer life was going to serve him well.

Unlike many who claim to be a believer, Daniel viewed prayer as an essential part of his life, not something that he could do when he was in trouble. He didn't see prayer as some "spare tire" that was only thought of when something in his life went flat!

Because of his devotion to the Lord, he is referred to as "greatly beloved" (Daniel 9:23; 10:11). It was Daniel's faithful walk and consistent prayer life that made him one of God's "beloved sons."

- *He prayed before every decision.*

One example of how Daniel viewed the importance of praying for wisdom was when King Nebuchadnezzar had a troubling dream. The Bible says that he woke up troubled and in a cold sweat (2:1). The king knew that dreams meant something and were considered very important. All of the king's magicians and astronomers could not interpret the dream or even help the king remember what the dream meant. They complained that his request was impossible; no one could do what the king had asked them to do.

The king was so upset with the wisest men of his kingdom that he issued a decree of death! Daniel was included with the rest of the wise men; needless to say, he was in a precarious position.

How would Daniel respond? Simple—he prayed!

While it's true that Daniel consulted with his close companions, he knew that the ultimate source of wisdom was God himself. A steadfast spirit will recognize that having wise friends is essential, but having access to the wisdom of God is imperative. Daniel was living proof of a New Testament truth: "If any of you lack wisdom, let him ask of God, that giveth to all men liberally, and upbraideth not; and it shall be given him" (James 1:5).

> *He answered and said to Arioch the king's captain, Why is the decree so hasty from the king? Then Arioch made the thing known to Daniel. Then Daniel went in, and desired of the king that he would give him time, and that he would shew the king the interpretation. Then Daniel went to his house, and made the thing known to Hananiah, Mishael, and Azariah, his companions: that they would desire mercies of the God of heaven concerning this secret; that Daniel and his fellows should not perish with the rest of the wise men of Babylon.* **Then was the secret revealed unto Daniel in a night vision. Then Daniel blessed the God of heaven** (Daniel 2:15-19).

Daniel was walking by faith and trusting that God would bring him the answer when he went before the king again. Faith believes God will work even when the answer is not readily available. With complete confidence, Daniel was able to tell the king's dream. Daniel told the king that no man could answer his questions or interpret his dream, realizing that what could not be done in the natural could only be accomplished through the God in heaven. "Daniel answered in the presence of the king, and said, The secret which the king hath demanded cannot the wise men, the astrologers, the magicians, the soothsayers, shew unto the king; But there is a God in heaven that revealeth secrets, and maketh known to the king Nebuchadnezzar what shall be in the latter days" (Daniel 2:27-28).

- *He prayed in the face of persecution.*

In Daniel 6 we see God honored Daniel because of his faithful and steadfast walk. He was now practically the second-in-command of the kingdom. Darius set over the kingdom 120 princes; and over these, three presidents, of whom Daniel was first (vv. 1-3). You can imagine how the other 122 leaders must have felt when an "outsider" was given such a place of prominence. They had to find a way to destroy Daniel before he exposed their corruption.

With the threat of the lion's den hanging over his head, Daniel did what he always did—he went to his place of prayer and talked to God about the situation. He didn't have to spend any time wondering if he should bow to the ungodly decree signed by the king (vv. 4-9).

All indications point to the fact that the wicked men thought they finally found a way to eliminate their chief rival to the seat of power. His enemies watched as Daniel made his way to his place of prayer and lift his hands toward heaven (vv. 10-11). Now they caught him red-handed, case closed!

How will Daniel respond? Will he give in and say, "Well, at least I tried," or will he take the politically correct approach and go on an "apology tour" and apologize to the other wicked leaders? NO!

Building Block #3—He was a man of *power* (6:16-23)

I am not talking about political or economic power, but an unassuming power that can only come when a person is fully confident that God is in control of their life.

He became a man who walked in the peace and power of God because in every circumstance he faced, including the den of lions, he remained consistent and refused to break under enormous pressure.

Look at the contrast . . .

- *There was no peace in the palace.*

Darius realized too late that he had been made a fool of, and there was nothing he could do to save Daniel. What a contrast between the two men. The king had no peace, was up all night worried, and Daniel was perfectly at peace with God and his new best friends, the lions!

- *There was perfect peace in the lion's den.*

Daniel was in a place of perfect safety, not because of anything he did, but because of who he belonged to. The Lord of the universe was there. While the most powerful man on earth, Darius, was powerless, Daniel received all the power he needed. So, I ask you: Who was the king, and who was the slave? Who was the one sleeping like a baby, and who was walking the floor all night? My guess it was Daniel, and not Darius!

According to the Bible, it was Daniel's faith and trust in God that saved him that night.

Daniel 6:23: "Then was the king exceedingly glad for him, and commanded that they should take Daniel up out of the den. So Daniel was taken up out of the den, and no manner of hurt was found upon him, because he believed in his God."

Hebrews 11:33: "Who through faith subdued kingdoms, wrought righteousness, obtained promises, stopped the mouths of lions."

The "secret" to his deliverance is no secret at all—it was his daily, steadfast walk with the Lord. Daniel could have taken the easy way out and just gone with the crowd, but he chose a different path. It is evident that Daniel would have rather been eaten by lions while obeying God's Word than do anything outside of God's will!

Daniel's accusers did not have a happy ending (6:24). As for the king—well, he made another decree: "Then king Darius wrote unto all people, nations, and languages, that dwell in all the earth; Peace be multiplied unto you. I make a decree, that in every dominion of my kingdom men tremble and fear before the God of Daniel: for he is the living God, and stedfast for ever, and his kingdom that which shall not be destroyed, and his dominion shall be even unto the end. He delivereth and rescueth, and he worketh signs and wonders in heaven and in earth, who hath delivered Daniel from the power of the lions. So this Daniel prospered in the reign of Darius, and in the reign of Cyrus the Persian" (vv. 25-28).

Think about this: It was one man's steadfastness, faithfulness, and power that led an entire nation to know the God of heaven. The next time you think your life doesn't matter, I urge you to consider the life of Daniel!

DISCUSSION QUESTIONS

1. Do you think Peter had Daniel in mind when he wrote 1 Peter 3:10-17? Read it and discuss.

2. Daniel faced real lions. Peter says Satan comes to us as a "roaring lion" (5:8-9). What is the similarity between the two?

3. Is it always God's will to save us from danger? If not, why not?

4. Why did Daniel make the choice to abstain from eating the king's food? What was the harm? Discuss in light of his refusal to "go with the flow."

5. If you found yourself in a foreign country, would you be the same person you are at home? Would you make different decisions if you knew no one would find out?

NOTES

1. James MacDonald, "Feasting on God's Word" (This article is an excerpt from the Bible study, *Authentic: Developing the Disciplines of a Sincere Faith*), *https://www.lifeway.com/en/articles/james-macdonald-authentic-feasting-bible-word* (accessed February 5, 2019).

2. A.W. Tozer, *The Pursuit of God* (Kindle Edition), *https://www.amazon.com/Pursuit-God-W-Tozer-ebook/*

Chapter 7

LOYALTY

Alexis Ibarra

This thou knowest, that all they which are in Asia be turned away from me; of whom are Phygellus and Hermogenes. The Lord give mercy unto the house of Onesiphorus; for he oft refreshed me, and was not ashamed of my chain: But, when he was in Rome, he sought me out very diligently, and found me. The Lord grant unto him that he may find mercy of the Lord in that day: and in how many things he ministered unto me at Ephesus, thou knowest very well

(2 Timothy 1:15-18).

The New World Dictionary of American English defines a *loyal person* as one who is "faithful to those persons, ideals, etc., that one is under obligation to defend, support, or be loyal to." It also defines *loyalty* as "the quality, state, or instance of being loyal; faithfulness or faithful adherence to a person, government, cause, duty, and so on and so forth."[1]

The virtue of loyalty has diminished in our culture, including the local church. Many view loyalty, commitment, and faithfulness as relics of the past; and no longer relevant, especially when it comes to relating to those who are in authority.

There was a time when ministry leaders viewed loyalty as a mutual affair. Loyalty was expected, not only from those who served in staff positions but it also flowed from the main leader down to everyone on the team.

Things have changed. And, it's not surprising.

The Apostle Paul warned Timothy about the dangers of the last days, and *betrayal (disloyalty)* of friends is at the top of the list:

> *You should know this, Timothy, that in the last days there will be very difficult times. For people will love only themselves and their money. They will be boastful and proud, scoffing at God, disobedient to their parents, and ungrateful. They will consider nothing sacred. They will be unloving and unforgiving; they will slander others and have no self-control. They will be cruel and hate what is good. They will betray their friends, be reckless, be puffed up with pride, and love pleasure rather than God. They will act religious, but they will reject the power that could make them godly. Stay away from people like that!* (2 Timothy 3:1-5 NLT).

After decades of ministry, I can affirm the fact that in some cases loyalty only extends to the boundaries of a job description. The mantra has become, "I will be loyal because I have to; if I'm disloyal, I will lose my job." It would be a great day if the church adopted the motto of the United States Marines—*Semper Fidelis*, which is a Latin phrase that means "always faithful" or "always loyal."

When I hire staff members, I have two qualifications at the top of my list: *godly character* and *loyalty.* If the potential hire lacks specific skills or education, I know those things can be taught. As long as they demonstrate godly character and value loyalty, I will find a place on the bus for them. I may have to rearrange the seating to accommodate their skill level, but they can ride along, receive the needed training, and help us accomplish the vision!

Dr. Richard J. Krejcir, in his article on loyalty, stated:

> *Loyalty is remaining committed to those whom God has brought into our lives and has called us to serve, even in times of difficulty. It is developing allegiance and respect in one another, and not seeking to manipulate the other person. Being loyal exhibits our commitment to Christ by our commitment—with discernment—to people and righteous causes at all times (Proverbs 17:17; Ecclesiastes 8:2-4; John 15:13; Romans 13:1-5; Titus 3:1).*[2]

Unless we are willing to exhibit loyalty and build a foundation of trust in our families, friendships, and ministry circles, we can't expect to receive loyalty in return. Galatians 6:7 says, "Be not deceived; God is not mocked: for whatsoever a man soweth, that shall he also reap." The law of sowing and reaping applies to everything in God's creation, including loyalty. If I sow loyalty, I can expect to reap loyalty, period; and if I sow disloyalty . . . well, you already know the answer to that.

I am not naïve enough to believe everyone is going to be loyal. It's in our fallen Adamic nature that wants to use, misuse, and take advantage of people. Climbing the ladder of success while stepping on someone's head is a common blood-sport, not only in Washington D.C., but, sadly, it has wormed its way into the foundation of the modern church.

Let's be clear. When I talk about loyalty, I am not talking about a type of "blind loyalty" that refuses to acknowledge when manipulation, abuse, and rampant immorality are taking place. So-called leaders who control their followers with religious-sounding words, like, "I am the only prophet who can hear and speak for God," or "I am the incarnation of Jesus Christ on the earth," demonstrate the fuel that demonic leaders employ. Men like Jim Jones, David Koresh, and Tony Alamo have used such language to keep their followers in line. That evil brand of loyalty is what cults are built on, and it must be confronted with the truth of God's Word!

As the Apostle James declared: "Who is wise and understanding among you? Let them show it by their good life, by deeds done in the humility that comes from wisdom. But if you harbor bitter envy and selfish ambition in your hearts, do not boast about it or deny the truth. Such 'wisdom' does not come down from heaven but is earthly, unspiritual, demonic. For where you have envy and selfish ambition, there you find disorder and every evil practice" (James 3:13-16 NIV).

The good news is, not everyone has unsavory motives or evil intentions. I have had the privilege of working with men and women who hold positions of leadership that understand the meaning of loyalty. They know that commitment is a two-way street and is a vital part of any ministry relationship. Such godly leaders have built among their team members mutual respect and loyalty that transcends petty differences and supersedes personal preferences. It's the right combination to make up a winning team!

One such leader is Alexis Ibarra.

Let me share a few snapshots of this extraordinary man.

Alexis was not always a part of our RIO Network. Early in his ministry, Alexis was a member of another denomination. But, he was told his vision for the ministry didn't fit with a certain number of high-ranking people within the denomination. He was informed that he was too evangelistic and mission-minded. He found it very difficult to function in such a restrictive environment. He felt his only choice was to leave and find a new field of ministry. He learned at a young age that in order to grow and develop his God-given potential, changes had to be made.

Enter Roberto Taton, our Latin American director.

Roberto was the first to meet Alexis Ibarra. Roberto discovered that rejection and disappointment had sent Alexis to a dark place. But, through much love, patience, and the mentoring process, this young champion began to blossom. The potential that was on the inside started to manifest on the outside.

I would not venture a guess as to how many churches Alexis has helped plant, not only in Panama but in the whole of Latin America. Alexis is also one of our top chaplains in the Global Chaplain's Coalition. He not only assists us in planting churches; he is a faithful husband and a pastor to a wonderful church.

Loyalty to Alexis is not just a word in a dictionary. It is something to demonstrate. He knows that actions are more important than words. His loyalty to me, and our vision, has been shown time and again.

For instance, there have been occasions where we have ministered in some of the toughest prisons in Central and South America; and then we turned around and met with a group of the most influential leaders in the nation to discuss leadership strategy. Whatever the need, big or small, his positive "can-do" attitude is always willing to roll up his sleeves and get the job done!

Because of Alexis' loyalty to the vision of our ministry in Latin America, he is now helping dictate policy and install vision strategy to reach more people with the good news of the Gospel. It takes that kind of commitment to expand God's kingdom. It's a beautiful thing to see loyalty working in a ministry.

My dear friends, if your passport to leadership is not "stamped" with loyalty, you won't go very far on your journey!

***

The Bible has something to teach us about loyalty. The Scripture is also quick to point out the dangers of disloyalty, and what it can do to a ministry team.

In Paul's second letter to Timothy, he highlights several cases where disloyalty crept into his ministry and affected his ability even to defend himself. Paul gives us insight into *three kinds of loyalty* based on his experiences.

1. Superficial Loyalty

In this personal letter to Timothy, Paul points out that there were those who either "turned away" from him or just decided it was time to "move on," and leave him. The core issue was their lack of loyalty.

*First, there were two men, *Phygellus* and *Hermogenes,* who will be forever connected to those who turned their back on Paul when he needed them the most.

"This thou knowest, that all they which are in Asia be turned away from me; of whom are Phygellus and Hermogenes" (2 Timothy 1:15).

As I mentioned before, there is a particular type of loyalty that only extends to the boundaries of a job description. This kind of attitude comes under the heading of "What have you done for me lately?" I have seen this kind of attitude before. As long as you can do something for them, and promote their ministry, they will stick to you like glue. But when the going gets tough, and sacrifices have to be made, well, color them gone!

Such was the case of Phygellus and Hermogenes. We know very little about them, but Paul thought it worthy of mentioning their name in the context of those who "turned away from me." Some Bible teachers have speculated that these two were a part of the leadership team in Ephesus who refused to come to his aid in Rome. For whatever reason, they considered Paul, a man who had labored among them for almost three years, unworthy of their loyalty.

Dr. D. Edmond Hiebert writes: "It would seem that Paul had written to Ephesus asking that some of his old acquaintances, men thoroughly familiar with his work and teaching, should come to Rome to testify in his behalf. But the apparent hopelessness of Paul's position and their fear of the possible consequences to themselves, had caused all of them to disregard the appeal."[3]

Still, others believe that these two were *in* Rome when Paul was arrested for the second time. When the charges against Paul were handed down, they decided it was too dangerous to stay around. Among the brothers, it was common knowledge that to align with Paul's ministry could cost you everything—not the least of which was your life. *One test of loyalty is what we will do when those we serve are going through difficulties.* The path of least resistance is to walk away instead of staying in the fight. Paul was in prison with a death sentence hanging over his head, so it was not time to ignore the man of God, but to stand with him!

"It has been their destiny to be handed down to posterity as men who acted an unworthy part toward the most noble man of all time in his extremity."[4]

*Second, is a man by the name of *Demas.*

"Do thy diligence to come shortly unto me: For Demas hath forsaken me, having loved this present world, and is departed unto Thessalonica; Crescens to Galatia, Titus unto Dalmatia" (2 Timothy 4:9-10).

Paul knew his time was short and he urged Timothy "to come shortly unto me." In our day, we might say, "Don't mess around, just hurry up and get here!" At the end of his life, he needed his son in the faith to be by his side— as soon as possible. Why? Paul indicated that everyone had scattered, except for Dr. Luke. He was practically alone, and time was short.

Demas is named *three times* in Scripture:

1. In Philemon 24, he is called a "fellowlabourer."

2. In Colossians 4:14, he is simply called "Demas."

3. Here in 2 Timothy 4:10, it is "Demas has forsaken me" (NKJV).

We don't have to wonder why he left Rome, because Paul said, "For Demas hath forsaken me, having loved this present world." There is no indication that Demas had deserted the truth of the Gospel, just that he found the "present world" more to his liking than the "promise of a future Kingdom."

First John 2:15-17 tells us: "Love not the world, neither the things that are in the world. If any man love the world, the love of the Father is not in him. For all that is in the world, the lust of the flesh, and the lust of the eyes, and the pride of life, is not of the Father, but is of the world. And the world passeth away, and the lust thereof: but he that doeth the will of God abideth for ever."

> *This does not necessarily mean that he attended places of worldliness, for it is possible to be a worldly Christian without ever participating in the world's pleasures. Worldliness is everything around us which excludes the Lord Jesus Christ. Demas probably began to adopt the world's standards; possibly he began to view missionary endeavour from the world's standpoint and found himself asking, "Is it worth it?" and consequently he lost the heavenly vision (Acts 26:19). It is sad when the world's icy grip begins to affect a Christian.*[5]

Demas is not the first, and won't be the last to deem their self-interest more important than sharing in the stress and difficulties of the ministry.

But, I have good news. Not everyone walks away! Not everyone leaves when the going gets tough. Alexis Ibarra is such a man. I have found in him loyalty to the cause of Christ that is above reproach, and transcends worldly comforts!

2. Subversive Loyalty

What do I mean when I say "subversive loyalty"? The word *subversive* means "to subvert or overthrow, destroy, or undermine an established or existing

system, especially a legally constituted government or a set of beliefs." Keep in mind the issue is always about CONTROL—always has been, and always will be.

There is a difference between *superficial loyalty* and *subversive loyalty.*

*A team member with *superficial loyalty* leaves at the first sign of trouble. When they realize there is nothing more you (as the leader) can do to help promote them, oftentimes they leave under the guise of "The Lord is moving me to a new field" (i.e., Demas moving to Thessalonica). They may toss a few bombs on the way out the door, but for the most part, they want out of the pressure cooker known as ministry.

*A team member with *subversive loyalty* is a different matter altogether. As the definition points out, to *subvert* something is to "overthrow, destroy, or undermine." This person has an agenda, and it is usually an undercover operation. On the surface, everything looks fine, and their loyalty is unquestioned until their real motives are revealed. I have found that pressure usually reveals and separates the wheat from the chaff! Underneath their smooth words of total commitment is a web of deception and lies.

The Bible is filled with examples of men who thought they knew better how to lead than the ones God put in charge. Author and Bible teacher Mike Murdock rightly points out that "the proof of loyalty is the unwillingness to betray."[6]

For instance:

- Korah gathered a team of core leaders and challenged the leadership of Moses (Numbers 16:1-3).

- Absalom used his charm and talent to steal the hearts of the people away from his father, King David (2 Samuel 15).

Below are two more examples of *subversive loyalty*.

1. *Hymenaeus* and *Philetus*, who infected the body of believers with false *(subversive)* teaching:

"But shun profane and vain babblings: for they will increase unto more ungodliness. And their word will eat as doth a canker: of whom is Hymenaeus and Philetus; who concerning the truth have erred, saying that the resurrection is past already; and overthrow the faith of some" (2 Timothy 2:16-18).

We don't know much about these two men except they were spreading false doctrine among the brothers. It seems only logical that these men were a part of the leadership team, or else they would not have been allowed a forum to teach. They were not discussing differing opinions about nonessentials but were spreading lies about the foundations of our faith.

To undermine the integrity of the Gospel (see 1 Corinthians 15:12) is a cause of alarm and must be identified, exposed, and stopped. Paul said that false teaching in the Church is like gangrene in the body that will spread, infect, and kill healthy tissue. If we don't take action and confront false teaching with the truth of God's Word, even good people are in danger of having their faith overthrown!

2. *Judas*, who revealed his subversion with a kiss:

"Then one of the twelve, called Judas Iscariot, went unto the chief priests, and said unto them, What will ye give me, and I will deliver him unto you? And they covenanted with him for thirty pieces of silver. And from that time he sought opportunity to betray. . . . And forthwith he came to Jesus, and said, Hail, master; and kissed him" (Matthew 26:14-16, 49).

For over two thousand years the name *Judas* has been identified with betrayal. He was an internal part of the leadership team of Jesus. He was on hand to hear every teaching of Jesus and witness every miracle that was performed. How much was Judas trusted? He was the treasurer of the team (John 13:29). To my way of thinking when you allow someone to watch over your money, you have given that person total trust. But, in the end, his subversive loyalty was revealed in the Garden, with no less than a kiss!

The question remains, Why? What caused him to cross the line? Why didn't Judas just pick up and leave— after all, others had done so (John 6:60-71)? Some have suggested that Judas was only "in it" for the money. I don't believe it was just about the money. If you read the Bible record, you will find that Judas had his ideas about how the

126

ministry ought to be run, and money was just a part of the whole list of frustrations that wormed their way into his heart.

Judas opened himself up to be used by the devil himself because he could never be satisfied with his part of the team. He wanted to run the show, and quite frankly, that WAS NOT in God's plan! When Judas saw that his intentions were known by Jesus, his decision to betray the Son of God was sealed for a mere thirty pieces of silver (John 13:21-30).

How sad to think that when team members don't get their way, they had rather tear the team apart and betray the leader than to deal with their simmering frustrations openly. The spirit of Judas is not born overnight, but I can attest from experience that it *will* manifest at a critical tipping point of ministry (Matthew 26:14-30).

3. Sacrificial Loyalty

> *The Lord give mercy unto the house of Onesiphorus; for he oft refreshed me, and was not ashamed of my chain: But, when he was in Rome, he sought me out very diligently, and found me. The Lord grant unto him that he may find mercy of the Lord in that day: and in how many things he ministered unto me at Ephesus, thou knowest very well. . . . Salute Prisca and Aquila, and the household of Onesiphorus* (2 Timothy 1:16-18; 4:19).

Paul referred to a man by the name of *Onesiphorus*. Who was he? You can tell something about him just by the definition of his name. *Onesiphorus* means "he who brings profit, or a profit-bringer," and he certainly became "profitable" to Paul.

By reading Paul's words, we can know several things about this loyal servant:

1. *He was not ashamed to be associated with Paul.*

"For he oft refreshed me, and was not ashamed of my chain" (v. 16). To not be ashamed of Paul's "handcuffs" meant Onesiphorus did not allow the potential danger to his safety or well-being stop him from ministering whatever comfort he could to Paul. What a contrast between those who turned away from Paul (v. 15) and this man who became a good example of loyalty.

2. *He was not a quitter.*

"But, when he was in Rome, he sought me out very diligently, and found me" (v. 17).   Onesiphorus left his home in Ephesus to find Paul even though he knew the danger involved. He could have made excuses, or he could have said: "Let someone else go, I've paid my dues." But he didn't. He made the dangerous journey to Rome and diligently searched for Paul, and found him.

3. *He will be forever remembered as a loyal servant.*

Warren Wiersbe writes: "Were it not for Paul's letter, we would never know that Onesiphorus had served Paul and the church. But the Lord knew, and the Lord will reward him 'on that day.'"[7]

Wiersbe is correct. The Lord knows all the loyal men and women who have sacrificed and served without recognition or applause. No doubt, without this book you would have never heard of a man named Alexis Ibarra, who continues to serve with dedication and loyalty. On more than one occasion, he has risked his safety and comfort to minister to me as we have traveled into some very dangerous territory. Onesiphorus brought a breath of fresh air to Paul, and I can say the same about Alexis Ibarra. He has often refreshed my life!

The reward of loyalty will be that day when Alexis and ALL of the loyal servants of Christ will hear, "Well done, good and faithful servant. Enter into the joy of the Lord!" (see Matthew 25:23).

130

DISCUSSION QUESTIONS

1. Think of someone you consider to be a "loyal" person and discuss how their loyalty is demonstrated.

2. Read 2 Samuel 15 and discuss the reasons why you think Absalom was disloyal to his father, King David.

3. Do you find that disloyalty is more prevalent in today's culture? If so, why? As Christians, what can we do to make it better?

4. Is there ever a situation where being disloyal is the "right" thing to do? Describe the situation and back up your answers with Scripture.

5. Do you agree or disagree with this statement: "If I am not loyal to God, how can I expect to be loyal to those who are in authority over me?" Discuss your answer.

NOTES

1. *https://www.yourdictionary.com/about/websters-new-world-college-dictionary.html* (accessed April 14, 2019).

2. Richard J. Krejcir, "The Character of Loyalty," *http://www.discipleshiptools.org/apps/articles/* (accessed April 14, 2019).

3. D. Edmond Hiebert, *Second Timothy* (Chicago: The Moody Bible Institute of Chicago, 1958) 47.

4. David Lipscomb, *A Commentary on the New Testament Epistles* (Nashville, TN: Gospel Advocate Co., 1942) 324.

5. *https://www.wordsoflife.co.uk/bible-studies/study-9-demas-the-snare-of-worldliness/* (accessed April 14, 2019).

6. *https://www.allchristianquotes.org/topics_detail/5423/loyalty/* (accessed April 30, 2019).

7. Warren W. Wiersbe, *Be Faithful* (Wheaton, IL: Victor Books, 1983) 135.

Chapter 8

VISION

Bill George

(1941-2017)

Where there is no vision, the people perish: but he that keepeth the law, happy is he (Proverbs 29:18).

The word *perish* in Proverbs 29:18 means to "cast off restraint," or better yet, to live without any sense of direction. It is a picture of a horse without a bit and bridle. Vision is the fuel that makes the engine of ministry roar to life and must be carefully maintained. Joel Barker said, "Vision without action is merely a dream. Action without vision just passes the time. Vision with action can change the world."

I agree with Barker's assessment completely.

Living with a God-given vision will give us spiritual insight to see what others cannot see, as well as the God-given potential of those around us.

One of the tragedies of the modern church is that many leaders are trying to lead by manipulation and control and not with a God-given, God-inspired vision. I have observed once-inspiring and powerful leaders wandering around, like the children of Israel, in the desert of discontentment. Why? Somewhere along the way, they allowed their vision to die a slow and painful death. Helen Keller was once asked what could be worse than being born blind. She said, "The only thing worse than being blind is having sight but no vision."

133

There are many reasons why someone may wake up one day and realize their vision is on life support.

Here are my top four:

1. *They allowed time to work against them and not for them.* Time is a neutral force. It can work for us or against us. If we are not careful, the passing of time can become a destructive force. As time "passes" and our vision remains unfulfilled, time will whisper in our ear and tell us, "Don't waste any more of your time, it's not going to happen for you." Or, you might hear, "You just thought you had a word from God; it appears you missed your opportunity."

We sometimes think that unless our vision is fulfilled by a certain age, it is not going to happen. I'm reminded that Moses was given a vision to lead God's people out of bondage at the age of eighty. And, who could forget that Caleb took his mountain at eighty-five! Gray hair (or no hair) is not a symbol of failure to fulfill your destiny.

2. *They listened to the lies of the devil.* One thing the enemy loves to do is accuse us of missing God's best for our lives. Lest we forget, the Bible says he is the accuser of the brethren. He will do everything in his power to convince us that our vision is only a figment of our imagination. He's a liar! "So the great dragon was cast out, that serpent of old, called the Devil and Satan, who deceives the whole world; he was cast to the earth, and his angels were cast out with him. Then I heard a loud voice saying in heaven, 'Now salvation, and strength, and the kingdom of our God, and the power of His Christ have come, *for the accuser of our brethren, who accused them before our God day and night*, has been cast

down. And they overcame him by the blood of the Lamb and by the word of their testimony, and they did not love their lives to the death'" (Revelation 12:9-11 NKJV).

3. *They became complacent. Merriam-Webster.com* defines *complacency* as "self-satisfaction especially when accompanied by unawareness of actual dangers or deficiencies."[1] That definition fits any leader who decides there is nothing more to learn, and no more territory to be taken. It is the attitude, "I've done my part, now let someone else do the rest." There is nothing more dangerous to your God-given vision than complacency!

Living with complacency will . . .

- Extinguish your passion, hence your vision.
- Cause you to settle for less than God's best.
- Develop a negative attitude toward change.

4. *They allowed distractions to divert their attention.* A well-worn tactic of the enemy is to cause distractions, to break our focus. The attempt is to move us away from our calling and our purpose. The Apostle Paul said: "Not that I have already obtained all this, or have already arrived at my goal, but I press on to take hold of that for which Christ Jesus took hold of me. Brothers and sisters, I do not consider myself yet to have taken hold of it. But one thing I do: Forgetting what is behind and straining toward what is ahead, I press on toward the goal to win the prize for which God has called me heavenward in Christ Jesus" (Philippians 3:12-14 NIV).

BUT . . .

Not all leaders allow their God-given vision to die. There are thousands of men and women around the globe who move forward in their vision every single day. They are the ones slugging it out in the trenches to reach as many as possible with the gospel of Christ.

Occasionally someone will stand out from the rest. One such visionary was Bill George.

From the very first time I had the opportunity to interact with Bill, I knew there was something special about him. John Maxwell said, "Leadership is influence, that's it; nothing more, and nothing less." If that statement is true (I believe it is), then Bill George is a prime example of effective leadership. Why do I think that about Bill? His vision consumed him. He not only *talked about* his vision, but he *walked* it out every day. He had the unique ability to "see" potential in someone who didn't see it themselves. Bill was a modern-day version of the sons of Issachar. First Chronicles 12:32 says, "And of the children of Issachar, which were men that had understanding of the times, to know what Israel ought to do."

Over his many years of service to the Church God, he stood out among his peers as a man with unique gifting, impeccable integrity, and immeasurable influence.

His roles included:

- A top-flight administrator
- A seasoned missionary
- A brilliant educator
- A prolific author
- A loyal servant in the kingdom of God

Time and space will not allow me to list the many ways Bill George made such a dynamic impact on so many

136

lives within and without the Church of God. But, I do want to point you to one particular award he was given by his beloved Lee University that sums up his contributions.

In 2014, The Lee University School of Religion (SOR) honored Dr. George as the department's Distinguished Alumnus for this year. An excerpt from the award will give you some idea of his far-reaching influence.

Dr. Terry Cross, dean of Lee's SOR, made the presentation:

> *"Throughout his ministry, Bill George has consistently mentored young ministers and missionaries," said Lee professor Dr. Thomas J. Doolittle. "He has dynamically impacted the lives of numerous pastors and ministry leaders who are serving the church in a variety of contexts."*
>
> *George currently serves as the editorial assistant to the General Overseer for the Church of God (COG). Previously, he has held pastoral/staff positions in Alabama, Florida, Texas, Tennessee, and the Bahamas, as well as various leadership positions within the COG. A Lee graduate, George has also served as an associate professor in the School of Religion, earning the Excellence in Teaching award.*
> *"I do not know any other minister in the Church of God who has directly influenced so many ministers through relationship building and personal interactions," continued Doolittle. "I am deeply grateful to Bill George for the energy and*

encouragement that he has extended to me and countless others throughout his ministry as a professor, pastor, missionary, mentor, and friend."[2]

My friend went home to be with the Lord on January 31, 2017. Although his physical presence will be missed, his spiritual impact will be felt for generations to come.

In writing about his home going, Dr. Timothy M. Hill, general overseer of the Church of God, said: "Today I lost not only my editorial assistant, but a very close and dear friend in Bill George. From serving as a missionary to serving at the highest levels within the denomination, Bill has always exemplified the true qualities of a servant. He was Church of God through and through, and was always available to take on any task assigned him—and he did it with a smile on his face and with enthusiasm. Through his superb writing and teaching, Bill George has left an indelible print on the Church of God. He will be greatly missed."[3]

***

As I said, Bill George was a man of vision. His ability as a visionary leader to "see" what was over the horizon and steer the course of his life accordingly did not make him better or more spiritual than others. Whether he was writing books or teaching a class, his goal was straightforward: *Impart spiritual insight to those around him to encourage every person to fulfill their God-given destiny.*

Living out your vision is not reserved for the "supersaints" or the "select of the elect." Not at all. A visionary leader is a person who is willing to invest the time, energy, and resources to see his/her ministry reach its God-given potential.

Below are three critical questions about vision.

Question #1. *What Does Vision Look Like?*

"Leadership begins with a vision. A vision is a clear picture of what the leader sees his group being or doing. A vision could be of health where there is sickness, of knowledge where there is ignorance, of freedom where there is oppression, or of love where there is hatred." [4]

A. *It's personal.*

As the old saying goes, "If you don't know where you are going, you might wind up someplace else!" A lack of direction stems from a lack of understanding of the vital importance of leading with a God-given vision. In other words, if leaders don't know where they are going, how can they lead others? It's like the blind leading the blind!

George Barna, in his book *The Power of Vision,* said, "Although they are good people and have been called to ministry, most senior pastors do not have an understanding of God's vision for the ministries they are trying to lead—and, consequently, most churches have little impact in their community or in the lives of their congregants." [5]

B. *It's powerful.*

A great vision will always release a powerful combination of creativity, innovation, and commitment. If the vision is right, two things will happen:

- It will create an atmosphere that will draw out the very best that people have to offer.

- People will be willing to make the necessary changes to make it happen. People will not change or adjust the course of their life for a small vision!

In his book, *Visionary Leadership,* Burt Nanus, observed:

A vision is only an idea or an image of a more desirable future for the organization, but the right vision is an idea so energizing that it in effect jump-starts the future by calling forth skills, talents, and resources to make it happen. For example, Henry Ford's vision of a widely affordable car and Steve Job's vision of a desktop computer for personal use were such powerful ideas that they were instrumental in assembling the investments and creative people necessary to bring them into being.[6]

Question #2. *What Will Your Vision Do?*

Consider the story of Joshua.

Joshua was in a frightening situation. He must hear from God, or all would be lost. Moses was dead, and he was the new leader.

A. *God's vision pointed Joshua in the right direction.*

"After the death of Moses the servant of the Lord, it came to pass that the Lord spoke to Joshua the son of Nun, Moses' assistant, saying: 'Moses My servant is dead. Now therefore, arise, go over this Jordan, you and all this people, to the land which I am giving to them—the children of Israel'" (Joshua 1:1-2 NKJV).

Think about it for a minute. His mentor (Moses) was dead, which shows us that no man is indispensable. Now it was up to Joshua to lead a nation of approximately two million people to the Promised Land. Not a small task for a guy who has been the number two man for the entire journey!

God did not leave Joshua without a fresh, powerful vision in which his fear and insecurity was dispelled.

> *"No man shall be able to stand before you all the days of your life; as I was with Moses, so I will be with you. I will not leave you nor forsake you. Be strong and of good courage, for to this people you shall divide as an inheritance the land which I swore to their fathers to give them. Only be strong and very courageous, that you may observe to do according to all the law which Moses My servant commanded you; do not turn from it to the right hand or to the left, that you may prosper wherever you go. This Book of the Law shall not depart from your mouth, but you shall meditate in it day and night, that you may observe to do according to all that is written in it. For then you will make your way prosperous, and then you will have good success. Have I not commanded you? Be strong and of good courage; do not be afraid, nor be dismayed,*

for the Lord your God is with you wherever you go"
(vv. 5-9).

B. *God's vision helped Joshua increase his potential.*

I don't know about you, but if I were in Joshua's shoes, I might be wondering if I could measure up to the task. But, one thing *is* true: Joshua would have never known if he could effectively lead if he didn't try; but he needed a fresh vision—and God gave him one.

God's vision will move us beyond our current circumstances to see ourselves in a new and different light. The greater the vision, the higher the potential for success. Each time we are faced with a new situation, we have two choices : (1) to stretch and grow to meet the challenge or (2) to turn away and miss out on a grand adventure.

C. *God's vision helped Joshua prioritize.*

Not only does vision give hope for the future, but it provides motivating power in the present. It did not matter if some of the people wanted to stay where they were, or go off in another direction. The imparted vision was for Joshua to head to the Promised Land—period. Once Joshua heard from God, his priorities were firmly fixed—not based on his opinion, but the Word of God.

The story is told about a missionary to Africa named David Livingstone. On one occasion, he had written to a particular missionary society in England asking for men to come and help him in his endeavor to reach Africa for Christ. In his request, he emphasized the number one requirement was they had to be men of commitment.

In responding to Livingstone's request, the missionary society wrote: "Have you found a good road to where you are? If so, we want to know how to send men to join you." Livingstone's reply came quickly: "If you have men who will come only if they know there is a good road, I don't want them. I want men who will come even if there is no road at all!"

There have been countless leaders whom God has used because they responded to His vision. A failure to respond to your vision will deprive those around you of a lack of leadership they so desperately need.

❖ Livingstone had a vision that all of Africa would hear the Good News, and it opened the door for thousands of missionaries to preach the Gospel.

❖ Noah had a vision to build the Ark, and he did.

❖ Abraham had a vision of a city not made with hands, and he looked for it.

❖ Nehemiah had a vision of a rebuilt wall around Jerusalem, and he built it.

❖ Solomon had a vision to rebuild the Temple, and he did.

❖ Paul had a vision to reach the Gentiles with the gospel of Christ, and it changed the world.

Question #3. *Are You Willing to Pay the Price?*

To order your life according to God's vision can be a challenging prospect. Why is that? There are forces within and without that want to do everything possible to stop us from fulfilling our purpose. The "vision thieves" are always at work trying to move us in any direction—except the one that God is taking us.

We must be willing to "count the cost" and move forward in our vision no matter the roadblocks that might be in our way. Jesus said in Luke 14:28-33:

> *"Suppose one of you wants to build a tower. Won't you first sit down and estimate the cost to see if you have enough money to complete it? For if you lay the foundation and are not able to finish it, everyone who sees it will ridicule you, saying, 'This person began to build and wasn't able to finish.'*

> *"Or suppose a king is about to go to war against another king. Won't he first sit down and consider whether he is able with ten thousand men to oppose the one coming against him with twenty thousand? If he is not able, he will send a delegation while the other is still a long way off and will ask for terms of peace. In the same way, those of you who do not give up everything you have cannot be my disciples"* (NIV).

Author and Bible teacher John Haggai said: "Having a vision is not enough. There must be a commitment to act on the vision. That is called a *mission*. There must also be a set of specific, measurable steps to achieve the mission. Those steps are called *goals*. Goals design the program for achieving the mission and thus fulfilling the vision. A leader will have one vision and one mission but many goals."[7]

Maybe you need to take a vision inventory and see where you are. Don't be afraid to be honest with yourself; remember. the Lord already knows what's going on in your life. Above all else, don't let your vision die—it's worth fighting for! It was Paul Harvey who said, "A blind man's world is bounded by the limits of his touch; an ignorant man's world by the limits of his knowledge, a great man's world by the limits of his vision." [8]

***

If you ever had the opportunity to be around Bill George (as I did), you were immediately struck by his confidence in God's plan for his life. Bill understood that before he could help, encourage, or lead others, he must first be clear about God's direction for his life. He counted the cost and was convinced that following God's will was worth every obstacle he encountered. Bill was sold-out to God's vision for his life, and because he paid the price of leadership, his vision became a magnet that drew others to follow in his footsteps.

DISCUSSION QUESTIONS

1. After reading this chapter, discuss your definition of a God-given *vision*.

2. Discuss the following statement: *A leader who attempts to lead without a God-given vision is destined for failure.*

3. Why was David Livingstone so determined to only have men come to help who were just as committed as he was? Is commitment really that important?

4. Based on the reading of Joshua 1, do you think Joshua was fearful of taking on the responsibility of leading the people? If yes, why?

5. What are "vision thieves"? Name them. What obstacles have you had to overcome to walk in your vision?

NOTES

1. *https://www.merriam-webster.com/dictionary/ complacency* (accessed November 1, 2019).

2. AUTHOR'S NOTE: You can read the full article of the award given to Dr. George *@http://www.leeuniversity.edu/ NewsItem.aspx?id=7097.*

3. AUTHOR'S NOTE: You can read the complete announcement of Bill George's death *@http:// clevelandbanner.com/stories/religiousleaderauthorbill- georgedies-at-76,51631.*

4. John Haggai, *Lead On!* (Waco, TX: Word Books Publisher, 1986) 23.

5. George Barna, *The Power of Vision* (Raleigh, NC: Regal Books, 2003) 31.

6. Burt Nanus, *Visionary Leadership* (San Francisco, CA: Jossey-Bass Publishers, 1992) 8.

7. Haggai, 13.

8. *https://www.goodreads.com/quotes/* (accessed November 1, 2019).

Chapter 9

TENACITY

Joe Mercer

And let us not be weary in well doing: for in due season we shall reap, if we faint not (Galatians 6:9).

The dictionary defines *tenacity* as "the quality or fact of being able to grip something firmly." It also means "the quality or fact of being very determined." Tenacity is a unique characteristic that is displayed by someone determined to reach their goal—no matter what obstacles are in their way. Perseverance, determination, and persistence all revolve around the same idea of recognizing what is essential and not letting go until the challenge is met.

In Matthew 13:44, Jesus tells a parable of the man who found a treasure hidden in the field. He said, "Again, the kingdom of heaven is like unto treasure hid in a field; the which when a man hath found, he hideth, and for joy thereof goeth and selleth all that he hath, and buyeth that field." Notice that the man recognized the value of what he had found and made up his mind never to let it go! That is the kind of example I am talking about when it comes to tenacity. Feelings become secondary to what you know, and the assignment always takes precedent and becomes the primary factor to the tenacious leader.

Oswald Chambers writes:

Tenacity is more than endurance; it is endurance combined with the absolute certainty that what we are looking for is going to transpire. Tenacity is more than hanging on, which may be but the weakness of being too afraid to fall off. Tenacity is the supreme effort of a man refusing to believe that his hero is going to be conquered. The greatest fear a man has is not that he will be damned, but that Jesus Christ will be worsted, that the things He stood for—love and justice and forgiveness and kindness among men—will not win out in the end; the things He stands for look like will-o'-the-wisps. Then comes the call to spiritual tenacity, not to hang on and do nothing, but to work deliberately on the certainty that God is not going to be worsted.[1]

I don't know many leaders who are worth their salt that are not tenacious. My fellow soldier and seasoned pastor Joe Mercer is one of those leaders who epitomize the word *tenacity* more than most. Joe knows what he is supposed to do, and nothing deters him from accomplishing the task. He is not distracted by political correctness, popularity, and other unimportant issues. One never has to wonder where you stand with Joe, especially when it comes to the Word of God. He is a Jesus man, through and through!

Despite many physical challenges, Joe Mercer displays the "bulldog" approach when it comes to his success in ministry. Whether he is preaching a crusade in Peru or ministering in a local church—nothing is going to stop him from getting the job done! Benjamin Franklin once said, "Energy and persistence conquer all things." Franklin's statement aptly describes my friend.

As long as this man of God has breath, he will be standing firm on the fundamentals of the faith. Joe has refused to bow down to the ever-changing winds that occasionally blow through the theological ivory towers of men who have nothing better to do than disparage the Holy Word of God. He is what we used to call a "meat and potatoes" man. A man that sticks with the old-time Gospel message—the same message Jesus gave in John 14:6: "Jesus saith unto him, I am the way, the truth, and the life: no man cometh unto the Father, but by me."

Time and space won't allow me to share everything that Joe and I have been involved in, especially mission trips. But, several highlight his tenacious spirit.

Several years ago, Joe and I were ministering in Juan de Lurigancho prison in Lima, Peru, which is one of the most dangerous prisons on the planet. We were setting up our sound system in a gym-like facility when we found ourselves in the middle of prison riot. Approximately six hundred inmates were playing soccer when a fight broke out. We only had two guards in there with us, and all they had were big black clubs—no guns. Well, you can imagine how nervous we were while those guards were pounding the heads of the prisoners with those clubs. At one point during the melee, Joe looked over and said, "Are we supposed to be here?" I said, "Yes, Joe, WE ARE supposed to be here!" To this day, that statement has become an inside joke between us. Since that incident in Juan de Lurigancho prison, there have been plenty of challenges that were just as difficult and dangerous. It didn't matter to him whether we were leading a large crusade or riding in a dugout canoe heading to some village in the jungle; the attitude is, "Yes, we ARE supposed to be here!"

We were in a particular city in Peru preparing for a large crusade. Joe took on the responsibility of taking pictures and filming a video so we could show the folks back home what we were doing . . . and hopefully, raise much needed mission funds.

While most of the team was getting some rest before the meeting, Joe was scouting out the best location to film that night. He decided to go up on the rooftop of a building overlooking the venue (where the crusade was to take place). Suddenly, there was a knock on my door, and I was informed that Joe had fallen through the roof; he fell almost four stories to the ground. I'm not sure how many bones were broken, or all the damage that was done, but I know that Joe had enough pins and screws in him to open a hardware store!

Much to our dismay, we had to leave Joe in a hospital that was not capable of doing everything that needed to be done for him. Even though he was in great pain, he insisted that the ministry continue that night and the days that followed. Eventually, we got Joe back to Tennessee where he could receive proper medical treatment.

That's the kind of tenacious attitude we all need. The attitude that won't quit or surrender to the enemy in spite of pain, difficulty, or hardships. We are in a war, a fight for our very existence; and Joe is an excellent example of a tenacious leader whose attitude is "We ARE supposed to be here!"

***

I can't think of the word *tenacious* or *persistent* without being reminded of an Old Testament figure by the name of Caleb. As we look at the life of Caleb, we can see a man who was persistent in his faithfulness to God and His word. As a result of his steadfastness, God blessed this man who would not give up or give in even when the "doubters" said it couldn't be done!

In Joshua 14:6-8, we read the account of the day Caleb asked for his inheritance: "Then the children of Judah came unto Joshua in Gilgal: and Caleb the son of Jephunneh the Kenezite said unto him, Thou knowest the thing that the Lord said unto Moses the man of God concerning me and thee in Kadesh-barnea. Forty years old was I when Moses the servant of the Lord sent me from Kadesh-barnea to espy out the land; and I brought him word again as it was in mine heart. Nevertheless, my brethren that went up with me made the heart of the people melt: but I wholly followed the Lord my God."

Caleb was now ready to take possession of all God had promised him through Moses. Caleb would eventually become a hero to all *mountain claimers* (not climbers) everywhere!

Let's look at three stages in this man's life.

1. He Was Faithful

A. *He was faithful in his witness* (Joshua 14:7).

Forty years old was I when Moses the servant of the Lord sent me from Kadesh-barnea to espy out the land; and I brought him word again as it was in mine heart.

When the Israelites came to the border of the land— the land that was "flowing with milk and honey"—they stopped short. We were introduced to Caleb when he and Joshua were commissioned by Moses (along with ten others) to spy out the Promised Land. Moses decided it would be best to "scout" the land to make sure it was everything God had promised. He chose twelve men, one from each tribe, to venture into the land and bring back a report. Caleb and Joshua refused to bow to the majority report.

*And they returned from searching of the land after forty days. And they went and came to Moses, and to Aaron, and to all the congregation of the children of Israel, unto the wilderness of Paran, to Kadesh; and brought back word unto them, and unto all the congregation, and shewed them the fruit of the land. And they told him, and said, We came unto the land whither thou sentest us, and surely it floweth with milk and honey; and this is the fruit of it. Nevertheless the people be strong that dwell in the land, and the cities are walled, and very great: and moreover we saw the children of Anak there. The Amalekites dwell in the land of the south: and the Hittites, and the Jebusites, and the Amorites, dwell in the mountains: and the Canaanites dwell by the sea, and by the coast of Jordan. **And Caleb stilled the people before Moses, and said, Let us go up at once, and possess it; for we are well able to overcome it.** But the men that went up with him said, We be not able to go up against the people; for they are stronger than we. And they brought up an evil report of the land which they had searched unto the children of Israel, saying, The land, through which we have gone to search it, is a land that eateth up the inhabitants thereof; and all the people that we saw in it are men of a great stature. And there we saw the giants, the sons of Anak, which* *come of the giants: and we were in our own sight grasshoppers, and so we were in their sight* (Numbers 13:25-33).

When the spies gave their report, it was not what Moses expected.

- The ten said: "We are not able" (13:31).
- *The two said: "We are well able"* (v. 30).
- The ten said: "We are grasshoppers" (v. 33).
- *The two said: "They are bread for us"* (14:9).
- The ten said: "There are giants in the land" (vs. 33).
- *The two said: "Their defense is departed from them"* (14:9).

What a tragedy!

With each negative word, they did three things:

1. They impeached God's promise—as if God would lie.

2. They impugned God's power—as if the giants were stronger.

3. They invalidated God's provision—as if God couldn't take care of them.

Caleb stood strong against the opposition, and despite what the majority said, he would always come down on the side of God's word. Of course, you know how this story ends. The children of Israel spent the next forty years wandering in the wilderness. They wandered around in circles for forty years until all of that generation died—

except for two men: Joshua and Caleb (see Numbers 14:29-30). After forty years of wandering and five years of war with the Canaanites, Caleb was ready to claim his inheritance.

B. *He was faithful in his walk* (Joshua 14:8).

Nevertheless my brethren that went up with me made the heart of the people melt: but I wholly followed the Lord my God.

There are at least six references to the fact that Caleb "fully followed the Lord." He faithfully walked with God even when the popular thing to do was to follow after the rebellious crowd (see Numbers 14:2-4). He never once stooped down to the level of the "haters" and the "doubters."

> *The word translated as "wholly" is worth meditating on. It is from the Hebrew word "Mille" and in this sense means "to follow fully," which is a verb meaning; to accept and follow leadership or guidance to the fullest extent. The word itself carries the meanings: be full, filled, fill, complete, finish, fulfil, perform, to satisfy, and carry out. It also carries a subtle meaning in this context of "eagerness to engage in some activity or event" (eager desire). When we consider the meaning and root of the word "wholly followed," it should help us to reflect on our attitude and heart towards God and His work, remembering Jesus' greatest commandment in Matthew 22:37-38.*[2]

2. He Was Fearless

> *And Moses sware on that day, saying, Surely the land whereon thy feet have trodden shall be thine*

156

inheritance, and thy children's for ever, because
thou hast wholly followed the Lord my God. And
now, behold, the Lord hath kept me alive, as he said,
these forty and five years, even since the Lord spake
this word unto Moses, while the children of Israel
wandered in the wilderness: and now, lo, I am this
day fourscore and five years old (Joshua 14:9-10).

A. *Caleb had God's promise* (14:9).

I cannot imagine how difficult it must have been for this faithful man of God to wander in the desert surrounded by such a defeated group of people. His body may have been in the desert, but his heart was already in the Promised Land!

There are times in our life when we must stand on God's promise even though it looks like nothing is going to happen. Everything about Caleb's circumstances spelled failure, but he would not give in to a negative attitude. That's the essence of tenacity and perseverance—not giving up when everyone around you is saying just let it go; it's not going to happen for you.

B. *Caleb had God's protection* (14:10).

And now, behold, the Lord hath kept me alive . . .

Some Bible scholars believe that during the forty years of wandering in the desert, there were approximately two thousand funerals a day! They fought battles but never claimed any territory. They wandered around from the borders of Egypt to the borders of Canaan, yet they never entered into the glorious "rest" promised to them—how sad!

157

Caleb was surrounded by death, defeat, and misery. But, in spite of all the hardships and pain, he never lost sight of where he was going.

3. He Was a Fighter

> *And now, behold, the Lord hath kept me alive, as he said, these forty and five years, even since the Lord spake this word unto Moses, while the children of Israel wandered in the wilderness: and now, lo, I am this day fourscore and five years old. As yet I am as strong this day as I was in the day that Moses sent me: as my strength was then, even so is my strength now, for war, both to go out, and to come in.* **Now *therefore give me this mountain,*** *whereof the Lord spake in that day; for thou heardest in that day how the Anakims were there, and that the cities were great and fenced: if so be the Lord will be with me, then I shall be able to drive them out, as the Lord said. And Joshua blessed him, and gave unto Caleb the son of Jephunneh Hebron for an inheritance* (Joshua 14:10-13).

A. *Caleb had a vision* (14:11).

Caleb had been to the Promised Land before—he knew what was waiting for him on the other side. His vision was not dimmed by:

- The wilderness
- His age (85)
- Lack of strength

Think about it for a minute. Here is this eighty-five-year-old man who some people would suggest he should be looking for a rocking chair. Instead of looking for a place to retire, Caleb is declaring that he is just as strong today as the day Moses gave him the promise of his reward. Wow! That's my kind of guy.

If nothing else, his story should be an encouragement to all of us gray hairs (or no hair) folks that it's not about the calendar, but God's timing.

Just because you have retired from your job does not mean it's time to sit on the porch and give up on your dream!

Psalm 92:13-14 says, "Those that be planted in the house of the Lord shall flourish in the courts of our God. They shall still bring forth fruit in old age; they shall be fat and flourishing."

B. *Caleb secured a victory* (Joshua 14:12).

Now therefore give me this mountain . . .

Just because giants were living on his mountain did not stop Caleb from attacking! Consider that Caleb took on the very giants that scared away the ten spies many years before. Caleb stayed focused on the power of God, while the doubters looked at the strength of the enemy and ran away like frightened children.

Joshua 15:13-17 records the result: "And unto Caleb the son of Jephunneh he gave a part among the children of Judah, according to the commandment of the Lord to Joshua, even the city of Arba the father of Anak, which city is Hebron. And Caleb drove thence the three sons of Anak, Sheshai, and Ahiman, and Talmai, the children of Anak. And he went up thence to the inhabitants of Debir: and the name of Debir before was Kirjath-sepher.

And Caleb said, He that smiteth Kirjath-sepher, and taketh it, to him will I give Achsah my daughter to wife. And Othniel the son of Kenaz, the brother of Caleb, took it: and he gave him Achsah his daughter to wife."

***

Like Caleb, Joe Mercer is a modern-day "mountain claimer." He has claimed many mountains for the cause of Christ. We need more men like him who, when faced with difficulties, chose not to retire but to re-fire his commitment to serve the vision given to him by God.

DISCUSSION QUESTIONS

1. Can you name a time when you felt your tenacious attitude won the day?

Describe the circumstances.

2. Read Numbers 13:25-33 again and discuss the reasons why the ten spies were so negative—especially in light of God's promises.

3. How did God honor Joshua and Caleb's faithfulness?

4. Do you consider age a factor in following God's will? Caleb was eighty-five when he asked for his mountain. Would he have been better off letting the younger generation take over?

5. Another example of tenacity is found in the parable of the widow. Read Luke 18:1-8.

   *What was she asking the judge to do for her?

   *Discuss its meaning in light of intercessory prayer.

NOTES

1. *https://utmost.org/classic/the-discipline-of-spiritual-tenacity-classic/* (accessed January 13, 2020).

2. *http://www.wwmf.org/2015/04/25/blog/daily-bible-notes/wholly-follow-the-lord/* (accessed January 24, 2020).

Chapter 10

FLEXIBILITY

Roberto Taton

I know both how to be abased, and I know how to abound: every where and in all things I am instructed both to be full and to be hungry, both to abound and to suffer need. I can do all things through Christ which strengtheneth me (Philippians 4:12-14).

Years ago, during a rather stressful situation, I was sharing my thoughts with one of my more seasoned leaders. After hearing me out he looked at me and said, "Pastor, always remember the forgotten beatitude." I must have had a curious look on my face because, before I could say anything, he said, "Blessed are the flexible, for they shall not break!" I have carried that piece of wisdom with me through almost every situation you can imagine.

Flexibility is an incredibly important leadership trait, especially if you are working in cultures that are not your normal setting. The "hardheaded" inflexible person on the mission field not only makes themselves miserable, but everyone around them is affected. I have discovered that if a person is going to be successful, and effective, there are times when you have to be able to back up and punt just like in American football.

If you want to know what it feels like to be in an uncomfortable situation, just plow ahead without a plan B in the back of your mind. Some supersaints think that making a contingency plan is not the spiritual thing to do. I can only speak from my own experience and say we don't always know what's best or why things happen the way they do. We have to be quick on our feet and ready to apply the "forgotten beatitude" at a moment's notice! The person who refuses to be flexible will always be resistant to change and will stifle the freedom one needs to follow the leadership of the Holy Spirit.

Marjorie F. Eddington writes in *The Power of Flexibility*:

> It requires flexibility (and grace) to stop or alter a certain course of action, to allow others to merge in front of you, to see a situation from another's perspective. Flexibility *may be defined as "capable of being bent, usually without breaking; adaptable, willing to yield; pliable. . . . Pliant stresses an inherent quality or tendency to bend that does not require force or pressure from the outside" (Dictionary.com). So, true flexibility isn't forced upon us (though sometimes we learn to be flexible the hard way). Flexibility is a natural quality that comes from within, from our true God-given nature.*[1]

The Bible pictures the child of God as many things. One of the most unique and beautiful pictures is that of a tree. And, not just any tree, but a palm tree.

Psalm 1:3: "And he shall be like a tree planted by the rivers of water, that bringeth forth his fruit in his season; his leaf also shall not wither; and whatsoever he doeth shall prosper."

Psalm 92:12: "The righteous shall flourish like a palm tree: he shall grow like a cedar in Lebanon."

The *Amplified Bible* gives more clarity on Psalm 92:12: "The [uncompromisingly] righteous shall flourish like the *palm tree* [be long-lived, stately, upright, useful, and fruitful]; they shall grow like a cedar in Lebanon [majestic, stable, durable, and incorruptible]."

Why are we challenged to "flourish" like a palm tree? Not only is the palm tree (more specifically the palm branch) a symbol of victory and eternal life (see Jeremiah 10:5; Revelation 7:9; Leviticus 23:40; Matthew 21:8), but a palm tree is a symbol of flexibility and strength in the middle of a storm.

Dr. Henry M. Morris observed:

The palm-tree figure is especially intriguing. In Scripture, the palm is always the date palm, stately and beautiful. It has extremely deep tap roots— called a root ball—and thus can flourish even in the desert, growing tall and living long. It is perhaps the most useful of all trees, not only producing dates, but also sugar, wine, honey, oil, resin, rope, thread, tannin, and dyestuff. Its seeds are fed to cattle and its leaves are used for roofs, fences, mats, and baskets. Its fruit is said to get sweeter as the tree grows older, and this is compared to the believer in a beautiful verse: "Those that be planted in the house of the Lord shall flourish in the courts of our God. They shall still bring forth fruit in old age; they shall be fat and flourishing" (Psalm 92:13-14). May God enable each of us to flourish like the palm tree—beautiful in the Lord, useful in

His service, bearing good fruit to His glory, even into old age![2]

Over the last twenty-five plus years I have had the privilege of working with many leaders that I consider "palm trees." Men and women who have learned to remain flexible in spite of hurricane-force winds that batter their ministries.

If I had to choose one word to describe our attitude in RIO missions, it would be *flexibility*. Here's what we've learned over the years: When the materials you need to complete a building project don't arrive—stay flexible. When cars or trucks break down, or get stuck in the mud— stay flexible. When a riot breaks out in the prison, and you aren't allowed to preach—stay flexible. When you break your ankle in a remote village deep in the jungle—stay flexible. Any leader who refuses to be flexible is heading for a breakdown of major proportions.

One leader that exemplifies the flexibility of a palm tree more than most is my friend and coworker, Pastor Roberto Taton from the nation of Panama. Roberto is a bishop in the Church of God, Cleveland, Tennessee, and oversees all of RIO's Latin American work. He has demonstrated flexibility as he traveled with me all over Latin America, parts of Southeast Asia, and the continent of Africa.

One of the most difficult places to minister have been the prisons. There are so many factors involved in just getting permission to go inside to preach the Gospel. Your flexibility quotient is challenged almost every time. On more than one occasion, Roberto has been by my side as we sat outside the gates of a particular prison waiting for hours just to gain entrance. During those times of stress, I never saw Roberto get upset, mad, or out of sorts. Like a palm tree he didn't break when adversity hit us.

Another example of Roberto's cool under fire was when he was being persecuted by someone who was an official in the denomination. Roberto did not retaliate or try to harm the person. He simply said, "If it's raining over here, I'll just step out of the rain, and move to where it's not raining!" He was saying that *if there is something difficult or negative happening in my life, I'm going to move to a more productive place.*

Roberto lives with a deep-seated belief that everything that happens in our life is "Father-filtered." He stands on Romans 8:28-31: "And we know that all things work together for good to them that love God, to them who are the called according to his purpose. For whom he did foreknow, he also did predestinate to be conformed to the image of his Son, that he might be the firstborn among many brethren. Moreover whom he did predestinate, them he also called: and whom he called, them he also justified: and whom he justified, them he also glorified. What shall we then say to these things? If God be for us, who can be against us?" In other words, God is not taken by surprise by anything that happens to us—good, bad, or indifferent.

Pastor Roberto knows that persecutions, storms, and upsets don't last forever because, in the end, God is going to work things out. His goal is always to help the team, no matter what adjustments need to be made. Even when it appears that nothing is going to work out, his "palm-tree spirit" rises up and says, "It is up to us to remain positive and flexible."

His positive attitude and flexible spirit has moved him to the top levels of leadership in RIO Network of

Churches. He is a vital part of RIO Missions as well as a board member of Global Fire Advance and the Global Chaplain's Coalition. We have been made stronger, and quite frankly better, because Roberto Taton is a part of our team.

***

Roberto Taton's flexibility reminds me of another man by the name of Philip. You see, it's not just when things break down and run off the rails that we need to remain flexible. There are times when things are going well and suddenly God interrupts what you are doing and says, *Let's go in a different direction.*

Flexibility is about making adjustments—a willingness to change your plans at a moment's notice.

Philip is first mentioned as one of the men chosen by the Apostles to help in ministering to saints in Jerusalem. Acts 6:5 says, "And the saying pleased the whole multitude: and they chose Stephen, a man full of faith and of the Holy Ghost, and Philip, and Prochorus, and Nicanor, and Timon, and Parmenas, and Nicolas a proselyte of Antioch."

After the death of Stephen (7:58-60), persecution broke out, and many believers were scattered throughout the region preaching the Word. Acts 8:1-4 says: "And Saul was consenting unto his death. And at that time there was a great persecution against the church which was at Jerusalem; and they were all scattered abroad throughout the regions of Judaea and Samaria, except the apostles. And devout men carried Stephen to his burial, and made great lamentation over him. As for Saul, he made havock of the church, entering into every house, and haling men and women committed them to prison. Therefore they that were scattered abroad went every where preaching the word."

On first glance it would appear that the church in Jerusalem was in BIG trouble. But, we don't see the whole picture. We have to believe that God has our best interest at heart even when the circumstances don't seem favorable. What possible good could come out of the death of Stephen? Not only his death but the threat of impending violence against the rest of the saints in Jerusalem.

Jesus had already laid out the plan to reach the known world with the Gospel: "But ye shall receive power, after that the Holy Ghost is come upon you: and ye shall be witnesses unto me both in Jerusalem, and in all Judaea, and in Samaria, and unto the uttermost part of the earth" (Acts 1:8). Is it possible that the early church grew a tad complacent with such overwhelming success in Jerusalem, and needed a not-so-gentle push to move them out of their comfort zone?

It appears so.

One of the early evangelists was a man named Philip. This is the same Philip who was chosen one of the seven deacons assigned to help in giving out bread among the new converts. Now, he was handing out the Bread of Life to a hungry city:

> *Then Philip went down to the city of Samaria, and preached Christ unto them. And the people with one accord gave heed unto those things which Philip spake, hearing and seeing the miracles which he did. For unclean spirits, crying with loud voice, came out of many that were possessed with them: and many taken with palsies, and that were lame,*

were healed. And there was great joy in that city (Acts 8:5-8).

Revival fires are burning. People are being saved, healed, and delivered. The joy of the Lord has filled the city!

But . . .

Just when the revival was spreading like an uncontrollable wildfire, the Lord laid His hand on Philip's shoulder: "And the angel of the Lord spake unto Philip, saying, Arise, and go toward the south unto the way that goeth down from Jerusalem unto Gaza, which is desert" (v. 26).

You will notice that Philip didn't try to talk the Lord out of His plan. I'm not sure if I were in the same circumstances, I might have tried to reason with God: "Lord, don't You see how many people are coming to know You? Are You really going to send me away to some desert place? You can't be serious!"

Not Philip. There was no hesitation, and no objection. "And he arose and went" (v. 27a). A simple statement, but pregnant with meaning. He simply obeyed the voice of the Lord. That's what I call *the essence of flexibility*—the Lord said GO, and Philip said Yes Sir!

I want you to see that things aren't always as they seem. What possible good could take place after leaving a citywide revival? How about sowing a Gospel seed in one person that will result in a revival that will eventually impact an entire nation? Every aspect of successful soul-winning is found in this exciting account.

I see three parts to this drama.

1. A Sinner Was Prepared (Acts 8:26-31)

Dr. Harry Ironside made an interesting observation: "Now you must not think of this as if Philip had just met a single individual driving a chariot across the desert. Undoubtedly what Philip saw was a great caravan—soldiers, merchants and all—and in the midst a chariot (which would stand out over everything else), the chariot of the treasurer of Candace queen of Ethiopia."[3]

A. *The eunuch was a responsible man.*

This was not some ordinary guy, but someone who carried great responsibility, and "great authority under Candace queen of the Ethiopians, who had the charge of all her treasure" (v. 27).

The Ethiopian eunuch exercised great power over the entire treasury of a country. We often think that those who carry authority and responsibility in the "world" would never listen to the Gospel message. Somehow we have convinced ourselves that only the "down-and-out" need salvation to the exclusion of the "up-and-out." My dear friend, all need Jesus—rich, poor, or in between. Never shy away from sharing the Gospel with someone just because they hold a fancy title!

B. *The eunuch was a religious man.*

Verse 27 says ". . . and had come to Jerusalem for to worship." He was a Gentile, not a Jew; more than likely he was a proselyte to Judaism. His desire to have a personal relationship with the God of Israel motivated him to make the long and dangerous journey to Jerusalem.

Many Bible scholars believe that the Ethiopian eunuch had been to Jerusalem to worship and attend the

Feast of Pentecost. Sadly, his hungry heart had not been filled by what he heard and saw in the Holy City. "The eunuch was one of those who looked to Jerusalem, for light and blessing and had gone there to worship. He returned, unsatisfied, still a seeker."[4]

2. A Soul-Winner Was Prompt (Acts 8:29-31)

Then the Spirit said unto Philip, Go near, and join thyself to this chariot. And Philip ran thither to him, and heard him read the prophet Esaias, and said, Understandest thou what thou readest? And he said, How can I, except some man should guide me? And he desired Philip that he would come up and sit with him.

A. *Philip was obedient.*

When God told Philip to go, what did he do? *"And Philip ran thither to him"* He didn't walk, all the while pouting—NO . . . he ran! I dare say, most of us would not have blamed Philip if he chose to ignore the Lord's direction and stay in the glow of a citywide revival.

Obedience and flexibility go hand-in-hand. We would be wise to follow Philip's attitude—his answer was always YES, even before the question was asked. The Bible is clear: "Behold, to obey is better than sacrifice, and to hearken than the fat of rams" (1 Samuel 15:22).

B. *Philip was observant.*

After listening to what the eunuch was reading, can you picture Philip jumping up to the side of the chariot, asking, "Understandest thou what thou readest?" (Acts 8:30).

I'm sure the look on the Ethiopian's face was priceless. But, he did answer the question: "How can I, except some man should guide me? And he desired Philip that he would come up and sit with him" (v. 31). Philip joined him and "opened his mouth, and began at the same scripture, and preached unto him Jesus" (v. 35). Oh, what joy and delight it must have been for Philip to have someone reading from Isaiah 53:7-8 and ask who the prophet was talking about. It didn't take Philip long to open the Word and show him Jesus!

3. A Salvation [That] Was Powerful (Acts 8:36-40)

And as they went on their way, they came unto a certain water: and the eunuch said, See, here is water; what doth hinder me to be baptized? And Philip said, If thou believest with all thine heart, thou mayest. And he answered and said, I believe that Jesus Christ is the Son of God. And he commanded the chariot to stand still: and they went down both into the water, both Philip and the eunuch; and he baptized him. And when they were come up out of the water, the Spirit of the Lord caught away Philip, that the eunuch saw him no more: and he went on his way rejoicing. But Philip was found at Azotus: and passing through he preached in all the cities, till he came to Caesarea.

A. *The eunuch was a changed man.*

The message Philip preached hit its mark. The eunuch accepted the truth of the Gospel and said, "Stop the chariot, I want to be baptized!" Philip said, "If thou believest with all thine heart, thou mayest. And he answered and said, I believe that Jesus Christ is the Son of God" (v. 37).

The proof of his salvation experience was not only his confession of faith, (see Romans 10:9-10), but in his

174

desire to be baptized. His immediate response shows that a change had occurred. A heart that was hungry is now filled to overflowing.

B. *The eunuch was a happy man.*

As they came up out the water, "the Spirit of the Lord caught away Philip, that the eunuch saw him no more: and he went on his way rejoicing" (v. 39). The eunuch no longer needed a prompt soul-winner to guide him, he now had the Holy Spirit living on the inside. For many years, men have derided the Gospel message as being too "easy," or too "simple." I am so thankful you don't have to DO ANYTHING to accept God's free offer of salvation (see Ephesians 2:8-10). The moment the Ethiopian eunuch opened his heart to Jesus, he was saved and became a new creation in Christ (see 2 Corinthians 5:17).

The eunuch traveled to Jerusalem looking for the one true God and found the city void of God's presence, and overtaken by religious exercise. But, glory to God, on his way home, in the middle of the desert, he encountered a prompt soul-winner with the good news of Jesus Christ. Is there any wonder he went on his way happy, rejoicing in what God had done!

***

Philip was no longer needed. "His mission was accomplished and now a miraculous event takes place. The Greek word for 'catching away' is used a number of times in the New Testament and means each time an action by power. The catching away of Philip after the work was accomplished is a little type of what will take place some day by the mighty power of God, when all the living

175

believers will be removed from the scene of their present labors." [5]

What became of the eunuch? Unfortunately for us, the Bible is silent on the matter. Some traditions teach that he went home and shared the Good News with the royal court, and a revival swept the nation. We just don't know. I am willing to leave it at that, and not spend time speculating.

Here's what I do know: One day when we will get to glory, we can walk up to the Ethiopian eunuch and say, "Tell us again the wonderful story of the day you met Jesus Christ on that dusty road." And, we can rejoice all over again!

177

DISCUSSION QUESTIONS

1. Discuss the following two questions:

    a. Why is flexibility such an important leadership quality?

    b. Where does flexibility rank among the other leadership qualities we've discussed in this book?

2. Can you think of a situation where you needed to be flexible? Discuss the circumstances.

3. What would have happened had Philip disobeyed the Lord, and stayed with the revival in Samaria? Do you think God would have sent someone else?

4. The Bible says, "The Spirit of the Lord caught away Philip, that the eunuch saw him no more" (Acts 8:39). He was gone—in an instant. What does that mean? Is this event a type of the Rapture?

5. Besides a palm tree, can you name another tree the believer is compared to?   Hint: Read Psalm 92:12 again.

NOTES

1. *https://www.biblewise.com/living/articles/the-power-flexibility.php* (accessed February 10, 2020).

2. *https://www.icr.org/article/believers-palm-trees/* (accessed February 10, 2020).

3. H. A. Ironside, Litt.D., *Lectures on the Book of Acts* (Neptune, NJ: Loizeaux Brothers, 1943; 1970) 192.

4. Arno C. Gaebelein, *The Acts of the Apostles* (Neptune, NJ: Loizeaux Brothers, 1961) 157.

5. Gaebelein, 159.

CONCLUSION

This book has been about insignificant people doing incredible things against all odds. Most of the people I've written about are like modern-day Nehemiahs who, just like him, declared, "I am doing a great work, so that I cannot come down: why should the work cease, whilst I leave it, and come down to you?" (Nehemiah 6:3).

A great work is normally defined by great obstacles. In Nehemiah's case, it was more than materials and inanimate objects. His great opposition, for the most part, was from people who were against Nehemiah's dream of rebuilding the wall around Jerusalem.

In *The Passport to Leadership* we investigate the principles behind what makes these leaders refuse to come down off "the wall" and focus, instead, on the opportunities before them.

If, after reading this book, you have felt the Holy Spirit stirring your heart, I have a question for you: Would you like to be a part of something bigger than yourself? Are you at a point in your life where you believe significance is something you want to pursue instead of success? If the answer is yes, you should give us a call and let's talk about how you can pursue your God-given dream!

Our contact information is below.

RIO MISSIONS
P.O. Box 887
Alcoa, Tennessee 37701

ABOUT THE AUTHORS

Ronnie Hepperly is president of Restoration International Outreach, which includes: RIO Network of Churches, RIO Missions, and the Global Chaplain Coalition. Bishop Hepperly is also superintendent of South East Asia for the Church of God, Cleveland, Tennessee, and director of Global Fire Advance (GFA), which is a church-planting initiative within the same organization. GFA is instrumental in planting thousands of churches yearly.

Bishop Hepperly and his wife, Jeannie, live in Friendsville, Tennessee, near Knoxville. They have two sons, Bryan and Hank, and five beautiful grandchildren.

***

Dr. J. Tod Zeiger has fifty years of ministerial experience. He is also the founder of the Joseph Institute of Leadership. He has led leadership conferences throughout the US, Europe and Central America. After his retirement from pastoral ministry he began working as a writer and a writing consultant for several well-known authors in the Christian arena. Dr. Zeiger and his wife Lorrie reside in Louisville, TN. They have five children and seven grandchildren.